SpringerBriefs in Political Science

SpringerBriefs present concise summaries of cutting-edge research and practical applications across a wide spectrum of fields. Featuring compact volumes of 50 to 125 pages, the series covers a range of content from professional to academic. Typical topics might include:

- A timely report of state-of-the art analytical techniques
- A bridge between new research results, as published in journal articles, and a contextual literature review
- A snapshot of a hot or emerging topic
- An in-depth case study or clinical example
- A presentation of core concepts that students must understand in order to make independent contributions

SpringerBriefs in Political Science showcase emerging theory, empirical research, and practical application in political science, policy studies, political economy, public administration, political philosophy, international relations, and related fields, from a global author community.

SpringerBriefs are characterized by fast, global electronic dissemination, standard publishing contracts, standardized manuscript preparation and formatting guidelines, and expedited production schedules.

More information about this series at http://www.springer.com/series/8871

Maxat Kassen

Open Data Politics

A Case Study on Estonia and Kazakhstan

Springer

Maxat Kassen
Eurasian Humanities Institute
Astana, Kazakhstan

ISSN 2191-5466 ISSN 2191-5474 (electronic)
SpringerBriefs in Political Science
ISBN 978-3-030-11409-1 ISBN 978-3-030-11410-7 (eBook)
https://doi.org/10.1007/978-3-030-11410-7

Library of Congress Control Number: 2018967747

This Springer imprint is published by the registered company Springer Nature Switzerland AG
The registered company address is: Gewerbestrasse 11, 6330 Cham, Switzerland

Acknowledgements

The author of the manuscript would like to express his gratitude to the Tallinn University of Technology for providing an invaluable opportunity to do research in Estonia and its employees whose welcoming hospitality and cordiality helped tremendously during his academic stay in the University in 2015–2016. In particular, he expresses his deepest thanks to Prof. Robert Krimmer whose friendly support and professional advices of a globally well-known expert in digital politics were truly crucial for the overall direction of the research in its early stages. Also, special thanks go to Dr. Ringa Raudla and Dr. Tarmo Kalvet, whose academic seminars and multiple brown bag meetings in the department helped to enrich generally the author's methodological approach to case study research. He also would like to express his thanks to Eva Õim whose intensive Estonian language classes helped a lot during his research and living in Tallinn in many aspects, making the stay much more productive and pleasant.

Contents

About the Author

Maxat Kassen is a Professor of Political Science in Eurasian Humanities Institute in Astana, Kazakhstan. He is a former Head of Foreign Information Service in the Kazakh National Information Agency—Kazinform (2003–2004). He is also a former Fulbright Visiting Scholar in University of Illinois at Chicago (2011–2012) and fellow of the Annenberg-Oxford Summer Institute at University of Oxford (2011). His research focuses on studying e-government technologies, globalization of open government and open data phenomena, digital politics, and digital diplomacy. He has more than 40 academic works on these topics published in various impact factor journals in the European Union, Kazakhstan, and USA and is also author of two books-monographs entitled "Understanding Systems of E-government: E-federalism and E-centralism in the United States and Kazakhstan" (Rowman & Littlefield Publishers, 2015) and "E-government in Kazakhstan: A Case Study of Multidimensional Phenomena" (Routledge, 2016).

List of Figures

List of Tables

Chapter 1
Open Data Politics: Building a Research Framework

1.1 Introduction. Setting the Research Agenda

1.1.1 Understanding Key Public Values of Open Data Politics

Before studying open data politics, all the more so in a cross-country and cross-institutional manner, one may ask what itself open data is really as a socioeconomic trend in government and, more importantly, why it is crucial to understand policies that help encourage its reuse by civic and private players to create new public services in digital forms. In this connection, the phenomenon of *open data*, which is also known as open government data, is usually defined by scholars as a combination of various formats and types of public information and datasets, such as statistical and contact data, archive recordings, geostationary and geographic information, government video, and audio and photo files, that are publicly available in special public digital depositories in machine-readable formats (Conradie & Choenni, 2014; Janssen, Charalabidis, & Zuiderwijk, 2012; Kassen, 2013; Kitchin, 2014; Safarov, Meijer, & Grimmelikhuijsen, 2017). Consequently, it is important to provide operational definitions to other no less pivotal and central elements of the related terminological paradigm, namely *open data platforms* and *open data-driven projects*, which are often defined as, respectively, public or semi-public digital repositories or portals that publish various types of government datasets in machine-readable formats (Charalabidis et al., 2018; Zuiderwijk & Janssen, 2014a; Zuiderwijk, Janssen, & Dwivedi, 2015) and third-party start-ups that are initiated and run by technically savvy citizens, independent developers, and open data entrepreneurs themselves, using such data as a raw material (Linders, 2013; Liu et al., 2015; Long, Zhai, Shen, & Ye, 2018; Zuiderwijk & Janssen, 2013).

Technically, nothing is really revolutionary in a simple fact that government information is now freely available in special public data depositories or portals. Actually, the publication of government files and anything that is related to the

M. Kassen, *Open Data Politics*, SpringerBriefs in Political Science,
https://doi.org/10.1007/978-3-030-11410-7_1

activity of public sector has always been regarded as a keystone of democracy and a main pillar of transparency in government. The two-century-long history of freedom of information laws is a realm that one should look at carefully to see the first instances of such practices in public administration. Later, the advent of computer technologies and optical scanners (Caldow, 2002) and, furthermore, the phenomenon of Internet in the 1990s merely made the publication of such materials and files easier, cost-efficient, and more productive (Tolbert, Mossberger, & McNeal, 2008). Even in the realm of electronic governance, a relatively new institute of public sector reforms, government information has always been regarded by practitioners as a service, i.e., a final digital product of innovative public administrators, *a certain thing in itself.*

What make the phenomenon of open data really unique today are its natural *raw materialness* and the fact that it could be operated in large volumes and, more importantly, in machine-readable formats since an extremely wide range of public information and datasets are generated in various government agencies and affiliated public institutions in a digital manner. Central, regional and local public agencies, schools, police, utility services, hospitals, environmental institutions, political parties, lobbying groups, central banks, semi-public corporations and companies, weather stations, state media conglomerates, army, special and intelligence services, etc. all these organizations generate a huge amount of information and datasets in various formats. Accordingly, the latest developments in information and communication technologies (ICT) that force the emergence of complex platforms, which tend to be interconnected with each other through centralized databases in modern digital government ecosystems in various agencies, are accelerating the process even further. This makes the analysis and processing of such new large volumes of government data not a trivial business anymore.

In this respect, President Barack Obama's executive directive on open government that he signed shortly after his first presidential inauguration in early 2009 was truly a revolutionary idea in the history of e-government technology. The memo encouraged federal agencies and municipal and local authorities in the USA and later governments in many foreign nations all over the world to harness the power of civic engagement and collective participation in developing independent open data-driven projects in order to accelerate the process and, more importantly, outsource the creation of many public digital services to civic and private providers.

Why was it truly a turning point in public administration? Usually, in accordance with traditional philosophy of e-government, digital services are provided only as a final product and in a really strict top-down manner, where the public sector is itself an initiator, developer, and promoter of almost all related technological platforms and projects. At the same time, the use of open data-driven government technologies is more collaborative and less directive. These technologies promote the development of various third-party platforms and encourage independent civic start-ups to reuse public datasets, which government agencies should publish first as a certain semi-product or raw material. Such reuse of data results in the creation of a completely new more collaborative model to advance

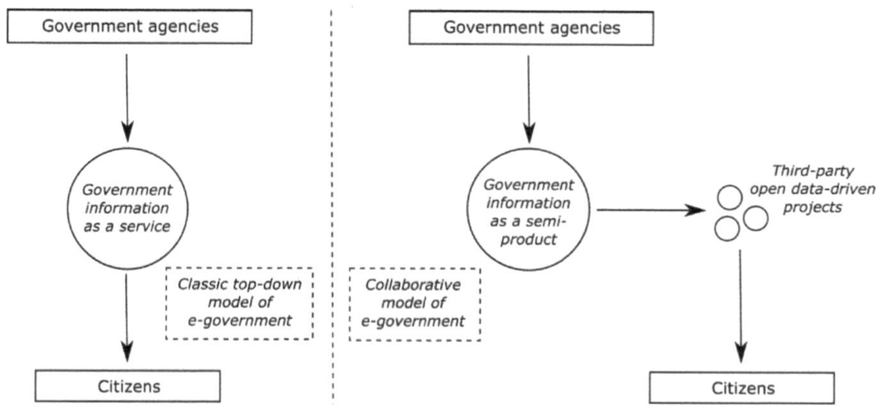

Fig. 1.1 Government information: as a service versus as a semi-product. *Source* Own illustration

e-government not as a service but as a platform to develop public–private partnerships and boost public sector innovations in civic communities (see Fig. 1.1).

In this respect, public sector presumably becomes not only more collaborative and participatory but also more cost-efficient and proactive since it is now playing a certain role of a special technological platform that provides government information and, more importantly, datasets as a free half-finished product rather than a final digital service, which is usually straightforwardly ready for public consumption, a result of understandably more expensive and time-consuming administrative process. Therefore, it would be more illustrative to conceptually consider open government data as *a certain prefabricated raw material.* This material could be further formatted and processed in various third-party applications, computer programs, and special hybrid mobile and online platforms without any copyright restrictions. The ultimate goal is to help the government to become more transparent, participatory, and accountable.

Open data has a great potential to boost digital participation among technically savvy citizens and independent developers (Brunswicker, Majchrzak, Almirall, & Tee, 2018; Concilio, Molinari, & Morelli, 2017; Hartung et al., 2010; Kassen, 2018a; Kitchin, 2014; Sieber & Johnson, 2015). Therefore, it is important to promote the policy agenda that would encourage not only public agencies but also other stakeholders from private, non-governmental, and civic sectors to join the movement and cooperate in a more transparent and collaborative manner. In this connection, *open data politics* is understood in this research as a set of policies aimed to promote open data as a common public value. These policies should be initiated, shared, and advanced by both the public and private stakeholders, especially in creating various third-party open data-driven products and services.

The public value, i.e., a main political and socioeconomic benefit or dividend of the concept, is that open data not only could potentially promote transparency of government, public sector innovations and generate new e-government services through the proactive publication of various data and its further reuse, but also make it presumably more open to civic engagement, public–private partnerships, and close networking with non-governmental and private sectors, especially in launching independent open data-driven projects. Moreover, the promotion of open government agendas, mostly reflected in the proactive publication of various datasets and public information and its reuse in third-party initiatives, could result in the advance of *digital democracy*, i.e., a political concept that propagates the use of new information and communication technologies to increase the level of participation from the part of local communities in public sector reforms (Mahrer & Krimmer, 2005), especially in relationship to the cardinal transformation of traditional communication channels that connects government and citizens in a more digital and interactive manner (Abu-Shanab, 2015; Gil de Zúñiga, Veenstra, Vraga, & Shah, 2010; Helbing & Klauser, 2019; Krimmer, 2012; Mossberger & Tolbert, 2010). *Civic engagement*, in this respect, is universally understood as a policy that is aimed at engaging a wide community of citizens to join a particular collective project or movement, which could result in the creation of public good or public values, contributing to its overall progress and development with their knowledge or finances (Chan, 2018; Chen & Reese, 2015; Mandarano, Meenar, & Steins, 2010; Smith, 2013), whereas *public–private partnership* is usually defined as the close cooperation between government agencies and various business entities in implementing or supporting public sector reforms or launching innovative projects (Das Aundhe & Narasimhan, 2016; Hui & Hayllar, 2010; Medaglia, Hedman, & Eaton, 2017; Sharma, 2007).

Therefore, hypothetically, all interested stakeholders, regardless of whether they are public agencies, businesses, non-governmental organizations, charities, independent developers, journalistic communities, or citizens, could directly reuse open data for their own purposes or, at least, easily contribute to its further development as a collaborative public project, which, in its turn, leads to the emergence of greater opportunities to promote new channels of political communication among peers themselves. In this respect, in order to better understand key public values of the open data concept, it is necessary to subdivide them into two main categories, namely political and socioeconomic. *The political category* should include such important public values as civic engagement and transparency in government since its increase could potentially lead to the rise of digital democracy and participation in the whole e-government ecosystem, i.e., resulting in certain political dividends for both state and society. *The socioeconomic category* should include such public values as public–private partnerships, public sector innovations, and new e-government services, where rise in the open data movement potentially indicates to the progress of information society and successful advance of public sector reforms in social and, less importantly, economic senses, i.e., resulting in certain socioeconomic dividends (see Table 1.1).

One can easily argue an understandably leading role of government agencies and independent developers as key players in these processes as the former publish such datasets in the first place and the latter reuse them then in their own open

Table 1.1 Categorizing key political and socioeconomic values of open data politics

#	Categories	Public values	Ultimate dividends
1	Political category	(1) Transparency in government (2) Civic engagement	The rise of digital democracy and political participation (political dividends)
2	Socioeconomic category	(1) Public–private partnerships (2) Public sector innovations (3) New e-government services	The rise of information society and successful economic implementation of public sector reforms (socioeconomic dividends)

Source Own elaboration

data-driven projects. However, open data politics turns out to be a multidimensional collaborative phenomenon, and publication of datasets is just the first initial mostly organizational and technological step of this multi-layer conveyor process, where the participation of other stakeholders is no less important, too (Kassen, 2017). *After all, the core potential of open data philosophy is fully realized only in a cooperative reuse of government datasets by civic and business communities.* In this regard, it is interesting to know how open data politics is promoted in a real-life context and, more importantly, how other stakeholders participate in the open data movement and what their actual input really is, taking into account the multifaceted nature of open data-driven government technology. The possible spin-off effects or actual public values or dividends of such innovative *open data-driven social networking* among government agencies, developers, citizens, businesses, non-governmental organizations, and many other stakeholders, which is reflected in the rise of government transparency, civic engagement, public–private partnerships, public sector innovations, and, finally, creation of new e-government services are what makes these phenomena so promising to observe and study from both political and economic perspectives (see Fig. 1.2).

1.1.2 The Key Purpose of the Research and Expected Outcomes

The key purpose of the research is to study a presumably universal nature of open data politics from a cross-country and cross-institutional perspectives in an attempt to understand the influence of political, socioeconomic, and, more importantly, cultural contexts on the development of the open government movement in

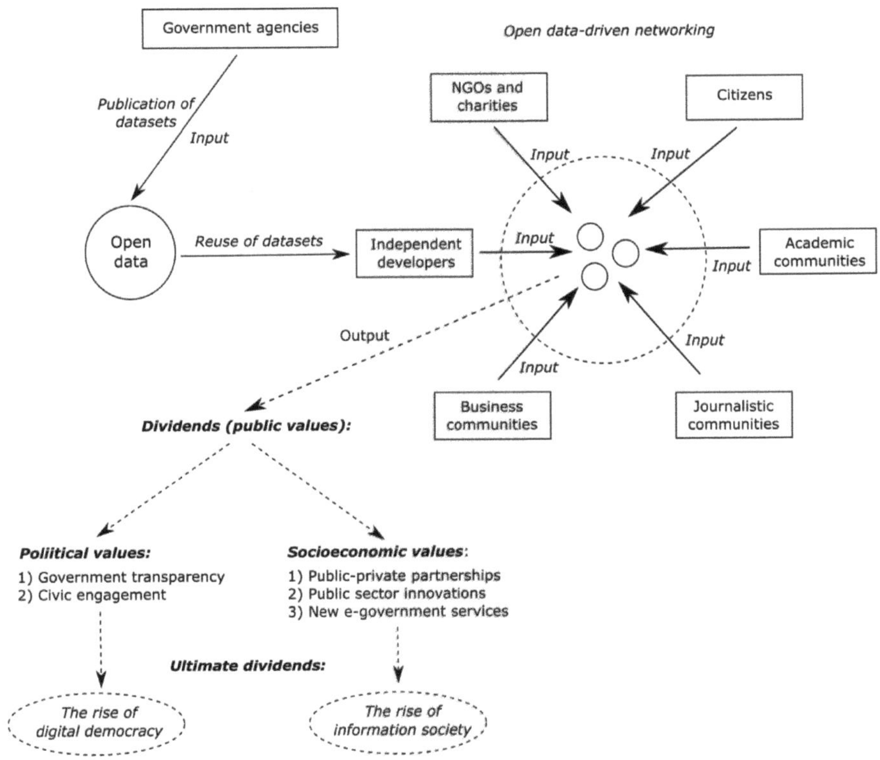

Fig. 1.2 Key public values of open data politics. *Source* Own illustration

countries such as Estonia and Kazakhstan, geographically representing, respectively, the Baltic and Central Asian regions and historically completely different traditions of public policy and public administration. In addition, by closely reviewing typical implementation strategies and tactics adopted by policymakers and practitioners in the area, the author of the book seeks to understand the potential of open data phenomena to boost transparency in government, civic engagement, private–public partnerships, public sector innovations, and new e-government services, regardless of different cultural contexts. One more goal is to locate main stakeholders, typical drivers, and challenges of open data movements by analyzing the operation of official open data platforms and various third-party open data-driven start-ups in these two countries so that to compare the results of the whole investigation and provide a set of policy recommendations for e-government practitioners, policymakers, non-governmental organizations, businesses, and journalistic communities on how to overcome the barriers and better harness the potential of the open data concept to accelerate socioeconomic development, promote participation, and, finally, improve democratic governance and advance information society (see Table 1.2).

Table 1.2 Understanding key purposes of the research and expected outcomes

#	The key purposes of research	Type of research	Expected outcomes
1	Study a universal nature of open data politics from cross-country and cross-institutional perspectives	Theoretical and empirical	Updating current knowledge to better understand the influence of political, socioeconomic, and cultural contexts on the development of the open data movement
2	Review the typical implementation strategies and tactics adopted by policymakers and practitioners in the area	Empirical	Understanding better a promising potential of open data phenomena to boost transparency in government, civic engagement, private–public partnerships, public sector innovations, and new e-government services
3	Observe and analyze the operation of various official open data platforms and third-party open data-driven start-ups	Empirical	Locating main stakeholders, typical drivers, and challenges of open data movement as well as providing a number of policy recommendations for e-government practitioners, policymakers, non-governmental organizations, businesses, and journalistic communities on how to overcome the barriers and better harness the potential of the concept

Source Own elaboration

1.1.3 The Theoretical and Practical Importance of the Research

The key value of the research is the presentation of rich empirical data and review of multiple demonstrative cases from the context of two observed nations. This could provide e-government policymakers, scholars, and practitioners with unique perspectives on how open data politics is promoted in a real-life context in a multitude of dimensions. This research presents a cross-country analysis that investigates phenomena of open data politics from multidimensional perspectives, in particular researching political, economic, and social aspects of open government movement in two different administrative and institutional contexts. The results of the analysis could help to understand better the potential of the open data concept to enhance transparency in government, civic engagement, public–private partnerships, public sector innovations, and new e-government services and identify fundamental ideological factors of the movement as a collaborative political and socioeconomic phenomenon, in which successful implementation could ultimately result in the development of digital democracy and information society. In this regard, the results of the analysis, which are based on the observation of rich empirical data in countries as diverse as Estonia and Kazakhstan, are intended for policymakers, developers, businesspersons, and specialists of public administration.

1.1.4 Identifying Key Research Hypotheses

Today, open data has become a watchword of technology-driven public sector reforms in global, national, and even local contexts and levels of governance. Being regarded as an arguably universal platform to increase efficiency in government and public administration (Huijboom & Van den Broek, 2011; Ubaldi, 2013) in virtually any country of the world notwithstanding, every nation has to apply its own strategies and tactics on how to better promote the concept (Davies, 2014), whether it is using official open data platforms as the only source of public information or resorting to the promise of public–private partnerships when both government and non-governmental sectors equally play a crucial role in the development of the phenomena. Likewise, the political understanding and legal regulation of open data phenomena may vary (Janssen, 2011; Nugroho, Zuiderwijk, Janssen, & de Jong, 2015), being considered as a platform to make government arguably more transparent in one country or as a focal point to boost civic engagement and collaboration in another. Likewise, different implementation strategies and tactics should reflect various political and socioeconomic conditions and priorities that the nations are experiencing on the path (Attard Orlandi, Scerri, & Auer, 2015; Gascó-Hernández, Martin, Reggi, Pyo, & Luna-Reyes 2018; Janssen, Matheus, & Zuiderwijk, 2015; Kornberger, Meyer, Brandtner, & Höllerer, 2017; Lathrop & Ruma, 2010; Lee & Kwak, 2012). Therefore, it may seem interesting to analyze how open data politics is initiated and promoted in different contexts, administrative, socioeconomic, political, cultural, etc. In this regard, the author of the book has chosen two transitional nations such as Estonia and Kazakhstan as appropriate examples for field studies and analysis in an attempt to understand what kind of typical drivers and challenges in political, economic, and social areas is associated today with the diffusion of open data, comparing the unique regulation policies adopted in each country.

The main hypothesis that helps to guide conceptually this research is that open data politics could presumably be regarded as a new socioeconomic platform to boost the participation of citizens in government. This could be done through various open data-driven projects and related civic engagement initiatives and through only which a collaborative and participatory potential of the concept could be fully promoted in administrative, political, technological, economic, and social domains. In this regard, it is important to understand what kind of related incentives the public sector sends to various stakeholders so that they would become more motivated to join the open government movement and reuse open data. In this regard, the study of various start-ups and initiatives that are being actively promoted currently in these two transitional countries and the analysis of key stakeholders' roles in these processes are of special interest in this research. The analysis of such stakeholder perspectives could provide a unique insider's outlook to the invisible mechanism of open data politics and related channels of political participation. Therefore, the results of field studies in 2015–2016, such as semi-structured interviews and personal meetings with various stakeholders, in each country helped to shed additional light on these assumptions with new perspectives.

1.2 Key Directions of Case Study Research

1.2.1 Understanding the Dynamic Nature of Open Data Politics

Open data as a political and ideological concept is at its infancy in practice and research. In fact, it was proposed as a tool of public sector innovations by Barack Obama shortly after his presidential inauguration in early 2009. His famous open government memorandum (Obama, 2009) has actually paved a direct way to popularize open data politics not only in the USA (Coglianese, 2009; Harrison et al., 2012a; Janssen et al., 2012; McDermott, 2010) but also in other parts of the world, leading to the creation and promotion of a wide range of unique federated and centralized open data ecosystems and platforms in many countries at both national and local levels (Akyürek, Scholl, Stodden, Siebenlist, & Mainka, 2018; Attard et al., 2015; Harrison, Pardo, & Cook, 2012b; Kassen, 2018b; Martin, Foulonneau, Turki, & Ihadjadene, 2013; Roy, 2016; Shadbolt et al., 2012). Not only most developed and democratic nations have initiated similar programs but also emerging and transitional societies in some parts of Africa, Asia, and Latin America decided to join the open government movement. They tentatively begin launching various open data projects and initiatives, encompassing political, social, and economic areas.

The globalization of open data politics and implementation of various open data-driven platforms aimed at improving government transparency and boosting participation of various stakeholders both public and private ones has generated a myriad of unique stories. These experiences shared by e-government policymakers, practitioners, and enthusiasts about this phenomenon are ripe for far-deeper analysis. In this regard, one of the primary goals of the research is to fill the gap in academic literature from both theoretical and practical perspectives. The extensive literature review recently conducted by Hossain, Dwivedi, and Rana (2016) on state-of-the-art in open data research shows that the cross-border analysis of the phenomena is an emerging area (Hunnius, Krieger, & Schuppan, 2014; Nugroho et al., 2015; Styrin, Luna-Reyes, & Harrison, 2017; Zuiderwijk & Janssen, 2014b) and there is still a shortage of empirical investigations and the analysis of the results from actual field studies, especially in transitional economic settings.

Most of the books in the area are focused on either economic, regulatory, or technological aspects of the open data policies (Gurin, 2014; Kitchin, 2014; Monino, Sedkaoui, & Lozzino, 2016; Morin, 2013; Mouromtsev & d'Aquin, 2016), which was one of the primary reasons to write this book in order to fill the gap in literature about open data, first of all, as *political phenomena*. Therefore, it is important to understand *comprehensively* open data politics in its real-life context and from many angles, e.g., empirical evidences and views shared by various policymakers, practitioners, and stakeholders both public and private ones and, more importantly, shed light on the dynamic nature of open data as a collaborative socioeconomic movement, especially on unique networking activities and trends that are generated in the area, ideally in all its diversity and extents. Furthermore, even though open data politics is beginning to play an ever-increasing role as an important socioeconomic factor of public sector innovations in both developed and developing worlds, there is a shortage of literature that explicitly investigates the phenomena in the context of transitional nations, since all works in the area tend to be studies that mainly focus on most developed and democratic nations of the world with a vast majority of case studies being focused on Western states (Alexopoulos, Spiliotopoulou, & Charalabidis, 2013; Alexopoulos, Zuiderwijk, Charapabidis, Loukis, & Janssen, 2014; Barry & Bannister, 2014; Bates, 2014; Bertot, Gorham, Jaeger, Sarin, & Choi, 2014; Bichard & Knight, 2012; Borglund & Engvall, 2014; Downs, 2016; Esteve Casellas Serra 2014; Hendler, Holm, Musialek, & Thomas, 2012; Huijboom & Van den Broek, 2011; Janssen & Zuiderwijk, 2012; Janssen et al., 2012; Janssen, 2011; Lassinantti, Bergvall-Kåreborn, & Ståhlbröst, 2014; Meijer, Conradie, & Choenni, 2014; Rohunen, Markkula, Heikkila, & Heikkila, 2014; Saxby & Hill, 2012; Shadbolt et al., 2012; Whitmore, 2014; Zimmermann & Pucihar, 2015; Zuiderwijk, Janssen, Choenni, Meijer, & Alibaks, 2012; Zuiderwijk, Janssen, & Parnia, 2013) and rarely on non-western emerging and transitional societies (Albano & Reinhard, 2014; Breitman et al., 2012; Craveiro, Santana, & Albuquerque, 2013; Davies, Perini, & Alonso, 2013; Saxena, 2017, 2018). In this regard, in contrast to traditional trends in academic literature, the author of the book studies the implementation of the concept in an unusual context, resorting to case studies of two emerging and transitional societies such as Estonia and Kazakhstan, paying special attention to the analysis of key drivers and challenges in the diffusion of the open data concept in an attempt to answer the ultimate question: Whether it is really harnessed by the members of civil society to promote civic engagement and transparent government there, i.e., political aspects of the phenomenon, or it is just an additional top-down tool of public sector reforms and e-government that results only in the advancement of socioeconomic dividends.

1.2.2 Setting a New Open Government Agenda for Practitioners

The study also claims to be an agenda-setting research that aims to provide a new perspective on the future development of traditional e-government systems through the prism of open data politics, which emergence as political phenomena could presumably change the fundamentals of governance, hypothetically making it not only more transparent and participatory but also more citizen-oriented, collaborative, and, more importantly, cost-effective by boosting public sector innovations and arguably even paving the way to introduce direct democracy. In this regard, one of the aims of the research is to generate policy recommendations for e-government practitioners. This counsel could help them to understand better what key drivers and challenges in political, economic, and social areas contribute to or hinder the diffusion of the open data movement as a cost-effective tool of *technology-driven public sector reforms*. The latter is understood in this research as a combination of administrative policies and strategies aimed at boosting public sector innovations through the use of new information and communication technologies. Consequently, one of the most important aspects in promoting open data politics, the concept of *e-participation* is defined as a political idea that intrinsically propagates the increased level of collaboration between government institutions and other stakeholders such as citizens and businesses, in related decision making in government.

In general, open data politics is consistently investigated in each of the two nations through the prism of public sector reforms in the e-government area, and the case study itself consists of three major steps such as the analysis of typical drivers, challenges, and identification of key stakeholders of the open government movement who play a crucial role in diffusing the concept as, first of all, participatory and, more importantly, collaborative phenomena. The key findings from each of the steps of the research and cases are synthesized and analyzed in the conclusion chapter and help to generate new knowledge and assumptions. In this regard, the ultimate aim of the whole analysis is to feel the gaps in the literature about open data politics in typical transitional settings, updating existing knowledge about drivers and challenges of open data movement and, finally, providing recommendations for e-government policymakers and practitioners who are actively engaged in the popularization of the concept. The book, which presents many ideas in an illustrative manner, could also be used as a material for collateral reading in various practical training and academic courses.

1.3 Understanding the Conceptual Frameworks of the Research

Taking into account a multidimensional and multi-institutional nature of the open data phenomenon, it seems logical to apply in this case study an unorthodox hybrid research approach, choosing the two most appropriate theoretical concepts for the analysis. In this regard, such popular conceptual paradigms in e-government studies as institutional and structuration theories are chosen for the investigation. They are used in different parts of the research as they ideally fit the case study that aims to analyze this complex phenomenon in all its diversity.

1.3.1 Institutional Theory: Understanding Different Administrative Contexts and Locating Key Institutional Stakeholders of Open Data Politics

The institutional theory is probably one of the most classic and popular conceptual approaches that have been widely utilized by a number of researchers to study technology-driven public sector reforms since the early 2000s (Barry & Bannister, 2014; Criado, Sandoval-Almazan, & Gil-Garcia, 2013; Fountain, 2004; Hassan & Gil-Garcia, 2008; Wang & Lo, 2016; Zuiderwijk & Janssen, 2014c). The key proponents of the institutional theory argue that it is important to study a new phenomenon of open data in its close relationship to the surrounding institutional and bureaucratic contexts that indirectly shape the course and pace of all public sector reforms in the area and adoption of presumably universal information and communication technologies in accordance with established organizational structures (Criado et al., 2013; Janssen et al., 2012). Moreover, taking into account the further diffusion and development of the open government concept all over the world and the arguable incorporation of various related collaborative digital platforms such as open data, peer-to-peer, wiki-based, and e-participation projects and start-ups, into its paradigm (Sivarajah et al., 2016), the institutional theory is becoming one of the most perspective ways to analyze open data phenomena as a truly collaborative project that incorporates various institutional stakeholders, whether they are government agencies, corporate structures, non-governmental organizations, mass media, developers, or citizens. In this respect, this theoretical approach could be helpful in understanding the universal multidimensional nature of open data politics from these perspectives, especially in locating key stakeholders of the open government movement.

1.3.2 Structuration Theory: Understanding Multidimensional Networking Phenomena of Open Data Politics

Anthony Giddens's structuration theory (Giddens, 1984) is another conceptual model that is widely used today in open government studies (Criado et al., 2013; Nam, 2012; Pawlowski et al., 2014), especially in an attempt to understand an ever-changing nature of technology-driven public sector reforms reflected in the emergence of completely new trends and networking technologies that now make scientists investigate the socioeconomic and even political implications of the phenomena post-factum and speculate dramatically on the complexity of the task to study them in a strong correlation with existing social structures. According to Puron-Cid (2013), the main advantage of the theory is that it helps to study public reforms in all their diversity, resorting to a certain epistemological flexibility in analyzing the emergence of complex networking social structures and human relations, the change of which presumably affects its development. Taking into account the fact that sometimes it is arduous to fully engage *a new open data-driven philosophy* into the established organizational structures, norms, and traditions of internal relationships (Faraj & Johnson, 2011), the adoption of theory that could help to understand the complexity of the concept and, more importantly, offer new ways forward on how to adapt them within the existing systems of public administration structures should be one of the most important directions in related case study research. In this respect, the structuration theory could be useful in understanding the multidimensional nature of open data politics in all its diversity, especially in observing a wide range of promising intra- and inter-institutional platforms in the area that help to network various government institutions at different structural levels. In general, the combination of these two conceptual frameworks helped to explore speculatively the phenomenon of open data politics in all its diversity (see Table 1.3).

In conclusion, it is necessary to note that even though a more detailed description of the methodology is provided in the following chapter, the use of these two theories provides a crucial guide to the theoretical aspects of the research in its different parts and is closely related to the key methods of analysis that is consistently applied in investigating all cases in each country. For example, the institutional theory is especially helpful in analyzing different political, administrative, technological, and socioeconomic players that may affect the development of the open data movement and, in particular, identifying its key institutional stakeholders who, for instance, officially distribute and technologically reuse the datasets, fund such open data-driven projects, or use the final digital products and services and provide feedback on them. On the other hand, the structuration theory may help to understand the open government movement in all its diversity, e.g., in political, administrative, economic, technological, social, and many other domains. It is especially useful to apply this theory in policy and networking analysis of open data movements in each of the nations, taking into account its multidimensional nature as a promising collaborative and networking phenomenon. In this regard,

Table 1.3 Conceptualizing research framework: theories, purposes, and perspectives

#	Conceptual framework	Purpose of research	Perspectives of research
1	The institutional theory	Understanding who are the key stakeholders of the open government movement	*From the perspective of different institutional stakeholders* in the open government movement
2	The structuration theory	Understanding the multidimensional nature of open data movement to boost networking among different government structures and institutions at global, national, and local levels	*Different structural levels* and various global networking projects in the area

Source Own elaboration

one of the most crucial parts of the case study research is the content analysis of various third-party open data-driven projects and start-ups, the full comprehension of which seems impossible without understanding how such collaboration and networking happens at different institutional and structural levels.

References

Abu-Shanab, E. A. (2015). Reengineering the open government concept: An empirical support for a proposed model. *Government Information Quarterly, 32*(4), 453–463.

Akyürek, H., Scholl, C., Stodden, R., Siebenlist, T., & Mainka, A. (2018, May). Maturity and usability of open data in North Rhine-Westphalia. In *Proceedings of the 19th Annual International Conference on Digital Government Research: Governance in the Data Age* (p. 18). ACM.

Albano, C. S., & Reinhard, N. (2014, September). Open government data: Facilitating and motivating factors for coping with potential barriers in the Brazilian context. In *International Conference on Electronic Government* (pp. 181–193). Berlin, Heidelberg: Springer.

Alexopoulos, C., Spiliotopoulou, L., & Charalabidis, Y. (2013, September). Open data movement in Greece: A case study on open government data sources. In *Proceedings of the 17th Panhellenic Conference on Informatics* (pp. 279–286). ACM.

Alexopoulos, C., Zuiderwijk, A., Charapabidis, Y., Loukis, E., & Janssen, M. (2014, September). Designing a second generation of open data platforms: Integrating open data and social media. In *International Conference on Electronic Government* (pp. 230–241). Berlin, Heidelberg: Springer.

Attard, J., Orlandi, F., Scerri, S., & Auer, S. (2015). A systematic review of open government data initiatives. *Government Information Quarterly, 32*(4), 399–418.

Barry, E., & Bannister, F. (2014). Barriers to open data release: A view from the top. *Information Polity, 19*(1, 2), 129–152.

Bates, J. (2014). The strategic importance of information policy for the contemporary neoliberal state: The case of Open Government Data in the United Kingdom. *Government Information Quarterly, 31*(3), 388–395.

Bertot, J. C., Gorham, U., Jaeger, P. T., Sarin, L. C., & Choi, H. (2014). Big data, open government and e-government: Issues, policies and recommendations. *Information Polity, 19* (1, 2), 5–16.

Bichard, J. A., & Knight, G. (2012). Improving public services through open data: Public toilets. *Municipal Engineer, 165*(ME3), 157–165.

Borglund, E., & Engvall, T. (2014). Open data? Data, information, document or record? *Records Management Journal, 24*(2), 163–180.

Breitman, K., Salas, P., Casanova, M. A., Saraiva, D., Gama, V., Viterbo, J. … Chaves, M. (2012). Open government data in Brazil. *IEEE Intelligent Systems, 27*(3), 45–49.

Brunswicker, S., Majchrzak, A., Almirall, E., & Tee, R. (2018). Cocreating value from open data: From incentivizing developers to inducing cocreation in open data innovation ecosystems. In *World Scientific Book Chapters* (pp. 141–162).

Caldow, J. (2002). Seven e-government milestones. In *Delivering the Vision* (pp. 35–56). Abingdon: Routledge.

Chan, M. (2018). Digital communications and psychological well-being across the life span: Examining the intervening roles of social capital and civic engagement. *Telematics and Informatics, 35*(6), 1744–1754.

Charalabidis, Y., Zuiderwijk, A., Alexopoulos, C., Janssen, M., Lampoltshammer, T., & Ferro, E. (2018). Open data evaluation models: Theory and practice. In *The World of Open Data* (pp. 137–172). Cham: Springer.

Chen, W., & Reese, S. D. (Eds.). (2015). *Networked China: Global dynamics of digital media and civic engagement: New agendas in communication*. Abingdon: Routledge.

Coglianese, C. (2009). The transparency president? The Obama administration and open government. *Governance, 22*(4), 529–544.

Concilio, G., Molinari, F., & Morelli, N. (2017, May). Empowering citizens with open data by urban hackathons. In *2017 Conference for E-Democracy and Open Government (CeDEM)* (pp. 125–134). IEEE.

Conradie, P., & Choenni, S. (2014). On the barriers for local government releasing open data. *Government Information Quarterly, 31,* 10–17.

Craveiro, G. S., Santana, M. T., & Albuquerque, J. P. (2013). *Assessing open government budgetary data in Brazil*. Paper presented at the ICDS 2013, The Seventh International Conference on Digital Society, Nice, France, March 1, 2013.

Criado, J. I., Sandoval-Almazan, R., & Gil-Garcia, J. R. (2013). Government innovation through social media. *Government Information Quarterly, 30*(4), 319–326.

Das Aundhe, M., & Narasimhan, R. (2016). Public private partnership (PPP) outcomes in e-government–a social capital explanation. *International Journal of Public Sector Management, 29*(7), 638–658.

Davies, T. G. (2014). *Open data policies and practice: An international comparison*. Accessed December 4, 2017 from http://dx.doi.org/10.2139/ssrn.2492520.

Davies, T., Perini, F., & Alonso, J. M. (2013). *Researching the emerging impacts of open data: ODDC conceptual framework*. Open Data in Developing Countries, Working Paper, 1.

Downs, A. (2016). *Addressing the open data mandate from the White House's office of science and technology: What does it mean for the USDA's economics, statistics and market information system?*

Esteve Casellas Serra, L. (2014). The mapping, selecting and opening of data: The records management contribution to the Open Data project in Girona City Council. *Records Management Journal, 24*(2), 87–98.

Faraj, S., & Johnson, S. L. (2011). Network exchange patterns in online communities. *Organization Science, 22*(6), 1464–1480.

Fountain, J. E. (2004). *Building the virtual state: Information technology and institutional change*. Brookings Institution Press.

Gascó-Hernández, M., Martin, E. G., Reggi, L., Pyo, S., & Luna-Reyes, L. F. (2018). Promoting the use of open government data: Cases of training and engagement. *Government Information Quarterly, 35*(2), 233–242.

Giddens, A. (1984). *The constitution of society: Outline of the theory of structuration*. California: University of California Press.

Gil de Zúñiga, H., Veenstra, A., Vraga, E., & Shah, D. (2010). Digital democracy: Reimagining pathways to political participation. *Journal of Information Technology & Politics, 7*(1), 36–51.

Gurin, J. (2014). *Open data now: The secret to hot startups, smart investing, savvy marketing, and fast innovation*. New York: McGraw Hill Professional.

Harrison, T. M., Guerrero, S., Burke, G. B., Cook, M., Cresswell, A., Helbig, N. ... Pardo, T. (2012a). Open government and e-government: Democratic challenges from a public value perspective. *Information Polity, 17*(2), 83–97.

Harrison, T. M., Pardo, T. A., & Cook, M. (2012b). Creating open government ecosystems: A research and development agenda. *Future Internet, 4*(4), 900–928.

Hartung, C., Lerer, A., Anokwa, Y., Tseng, C., Brunette, W., & Borriello, G. (2010, December). Open data kit: Tools to build information services for developing regions. In *Proceedings of the 4th ACM/IEEE International Conference on Information and Communication Technologies and Development* (p. 18). ACM.

Hassan, S., & Gil-Garcia, J. R. (2008). *Institutional theory and e-government research*. Handbook of research on public information technology, 1.

Helbing, D., & Klauser, S. (2019). How to make democracy work in the digital age. In *Towards Digital Enlightenment* (pp. 157–162). Cham: Springer.

Hendler, J., Holm, J., Musialek, C., & Thomas, G. (2012). US government linked open data: Semantic.data.gov. *IEEE Intelligent Systems, 27*(3), 25–31.
Hossain, M. A., Dwivedi, Y. K., & Rana, N. P. (2016). State-of-the-art in open data research: Insights from existing literature and a research agenda. *Journal of organizational computing and electronic commerce, 26*(1–2), 14–40.
Hui, G., & Hayllar, M. R. (2010). Creating public value in e-Government: A public-private-citizen collaboration framework in Web 2.0. *Australian Journal of Public Administration, 69,* 120–131.
Huijboom, N., & Van den Broek, T. (2011). Open data: An international comparison of strategies. *European Journal of ePractice, 12*(1), 1–13.
Hunnius, S., Krieger, B., & Schuppan, T. (2014, September). Providing, guarding, shielding: Open government data in Spain and Germany. In *2014 EGPA Annual Conference*, September 10–12, 2014 in Speyer, Germany.
Janssen, K. (2011). The influence of the PSI directive on open government data: An overview of recent developments. *Government Information Quarterly, 28*(4), 446–456.
Janssen, M., & Zuiderwijk, A. (2012, May). Open data and transformational government. In *Transforming Government Workshop*. Brunel University, United Kingdom.
Janssen, M., Charalabidis, Y., & Zuiderwijk, A. (2012). Benefits, adoption barriers and myths of open data and open government. *Information Systems Management, 29*(4), 258–268.
Janssen, M., Matheus, R., & Zuiderwijk, A. (2015, August). Big and open linked data (BOLD) to create smart cities and citizens: Insights from smart energy and mobility cases. In *International Conference on Electronic Government* (pp. 79–90). Cham: Springer.
Kassen, M. (2013). A promising phenomenon of open data: A case study of the Chicago open data project. *Government Information Quarterly, 30*(4), 508–513.
Kassen, M. (2017). Understanding transparency of government from a Nordic perspective: Open government and open data movement as a multidimensional collaborative phenomenon in Sweden. *Journal of Global Information Technology Management, 20*(4), 236–275.
Kassen, M. (2018a). Open data and its intermediaries: A cross-country perspective on participatory movement among independent developers. *Knowledge Management Research & Practice, 16* (3), 327–342.
Kassen, M. (2018b). Open data and its institutional ecosystems: A comparative cross-jurisdictional analysis of open data platforms. *Canadian Public Administration, 61*(1), 109–129.
Kitchin, R. (2014). *The data revolution: Big data, open data, data infrastructures and their consequences*. Thousand Oaks: Sage.
Kornberger, M., Meyer, R. E., Brandtner, C., & Höllerer, M. A. (2017). When bureaucracy meets the crowd: Studying "open government" in the Vienna City Administration. *Organization Studies, 38*(2), 179–200.
Krimmer, R. (2012). *The evolution of e-voting: Why voting technology is used and how it affects democracy* (Doctoral Theses Series I: Social Sciences). Tallinn University of Technology, 19.
Lassinantti, J., Bergvall-Kåreborn, B., & Ståhlbröst, A. (2014). Shaping local open data initiatives: Politics and implications. *Journal of Theoretical and Applied Electronic Commerce Research, 9*(2), 17–33.
Lathrop, D., & Ruma, L. (2010). *Open government: Collaboration, transparency, and participation in practice*. MA: O'Reilly Media Inc.
Lee, G., & Kwak, Y. H. (2012). An open government maturity model for social media-based public engagement. *Government Information Quarterly, 29*(4), 492–503.
Linders, D. (2013). Towards open development: Leveraging open data to improve the planning and coordination of international aid. *Government Information Quarterly, 30*(4), 426–434.
Liu, X., Song, Y., Wu, K., Wang, J., Li, D., & Long, Y. (2015). Understanding urban China with open data. *Cities, 47,* 53–61.
Long, Y., Zhai, W., Shen, Y., & Ye, X. (2018). Understanding uneven urban expansion with natural cities using open data. *Landscape and Urban Planning, 177,* 281–293.
Mahrer, H., & Krimmer, R. (2005). Towards the enhancement of e-democracy: Identifying the notion of the 'middleman paradox'. *Information Systems Journal, 15*(1), 27–42.

Mandarano, L., Meenar, M., & Steins, C. (2010). Building social capital in the digital age of civic engagement. *Journal of Planning Literature, 25*(2), 123–135.
Martin, S., Foulonneau, M., Turki, S., & Ihadjadene, M. (2013, June). Open data: Barriers, risks and opportunities. In *Proceedings of the 13th European Conference on eGovernment: ECEG* (pp. 301–309).
McDermott, P. (2010). Building open government. *Government Information Quarterly, 27*(4), 401–413.
Medaglia, R., Hedman, J., & Eaton, B. (2017). *Public-private collaboration in the emergence of a national electronic identification policy: The case of NemID in Denmark.*
Meijer, R., Conradie, P., & Choenni, S. (2014). Reconciling contradictions of open data regarding transparency, privacy, security and trust. *Journal of Theoretical and Applied Electronic Commerce Research, 9*(3), 32–44.
Monino, J. L., Sedkaoui, S., & Lozzino, A. (2016). *Big data, open data and data development* (Vol. 3). Hoboken: Wiley.
Morin, P. (2013). *Open data structures: An introduction* (Vol. 2). Canada: Athabasca University Press.
Mossberger, K., & Tolbert, C. J. (2010). Digital democracy: How politics online is changing electoral participation. In *The Oxford handbook of American elections and political behavior.* Oxford: Oxford University Press.
Mouromtsev, D., & d'Aquin, M. (Eds.). (2016). *Open data for education: Linked, shared, and reusable data for teaching and learning (Vol. 9500).* Berlin: Springer.
Nam, T. (2012). Citizens' attitudes toward open government and government 2.0. *International Review of Administrative Sciences, 78*(2), 346–368.
Nugroho, R. P., Zuiderwijk, A., Janssen, M., & de Jong, M. (2015). A comparison of national open data policies: Lessons learned. *Transforming Government: People, Process and Policy, 9* (3), 286–308.
Obama, B. (2009). *Transparency and open government. Memorandum for the heads of executive departments and agencies.* The White House. Washington, DC.
Pawlowski, J. M., Bick, M., Peinl, R., Thalmann, S., Maier, R., Hetmank, D. W. I. L. … Pirkkalainen, H. (2014). Social knowledge environments. *Business & Information Systems Engineering, 6*(2), 81–88.
Puron-Cid, G. (2013). Interdisciplinary application of structuration theory for e-government: A case study of an IT-enabled budget reform. *Government Information Quarterly, 30,* S46–S58.
Rohunen, A., Markkula, J., Heikkila, M., & Heikkila, J. (2014). Open traffic data for future service innovation: Addressing the privacy challenges of driving data. *Journal of Theoretical and Applied Electronic Commerce Research, 9*(3), 71–89.
Roy, J. (2016). Data, dialogue, and innovation: Opportunities and challenges for "Open Government" in Canada. *Journal of Innovation Management, 4*(1), 22–38.
Safarov, I., Meijer, A., & Grimmelikhuijsen, S. (2017). Utilization of open government data: A systematic literature review of types, conditions, effects and users. *Information Polity, 22*(1), 1–24.
Saxby, S., & Hill, C. (2012). Public sector information and open data: Which way forward for the UK? *International Journal of Public Law and Policy, 2*(3), 299–333.
Saxena, S. (2017). Open data in Israel, Georgia and Uzbekistan: Nature and scope. *Information and Learning Science, 118*(7/8), 406–419.
Saxena, S. (2018). Open government data (OGD) in six Middle East countries: An evaluation of the national open data portals. *Digital Policy, Regulation and Governance, 20*(4).
Shadbolt, N., O'Hara, K., Berners-Lee, T., Gibbins, N., Glaser, H., & Hall, W. (2012). Linked open government data: Lessons from data.gov.uk. *IEEE Intelligent Systems, 27*(3), 16–24.
Sharma, S. (2007). Exploring best practices in public–private partnership (PPP) in e-Government through select Asian case studies. *The International Information & Library Review, 39*(3–4), 203–210.
Sieber, R. E., & Johnson, P. A. (2015). Civic open data at a crossroads: Dominant models and current challenges. *Government Information Quarterly, 32*(3), 308–315.

Sivarajah, U., Weerakkody, V., Waller, P., Lee, H., Irani, Z., Choi, Y. … Glikman, Y. (2016). The role of e-participation and open data in evidence-based policy decision making in local government. *Journal of Organizational Computing and Electronic Commerce, 26*(1–2), 64–79.
Smith, A. (2013). Civic engagement in the digital age. *Pew Research Center, 25,* 307–332.
Styrin, E., Luna-Reyes, L. F., & Harrison, T. M. (2017). Open data ecosystems: An international comparison. *Transforming Government: People, Process and Policy, 11*(1), 132–156.
Tolbert, C. J., Mossberger, K., & McNeal, R. (2008). Institutions, policy innovation, and E-Government in the American States. *Public Administration Review, 68*(3), 549–563.
Ubaldi, B. (2013). Open government data. Accessed December 4, 2017 from http://www.oecd-ilibrary.org/governance/open-government-data_5k46bj4f03s7-en.
Wang, H. J., & Lo, J. (2016). Adoption of open government data among government agencies. *Government Information Quarterly, 33*(1), 80–88.
Whitmore, A. (2014). Using open government data to predict war: A case study of data and systems challenges. *Government Information Quarterly, 31*(4), 622–630.
Zimmermann, H. D., & Pucihar, A. (2015). Open innovation, open data and new business models. In *Open Data and New Business Models*, September 1, 2015.
Zuiderwijk, A., & Janssen, M. (2013, September). A coordination theory perspective to improve the use of open data in policy-making. In *International Conference on Electronic Government* (pp. 38–49). Berlin, Heidelberg: Springer.
Zuiderwijk, A., & Janssen, M. (2014a). Barriers and development directions for the publication and usage of open data: A socio-technical view. In *Open Government* (pp. 115–135). New York, NY: Springer.
Zuiderwijk, A., & Janssen, M. (2014b). Open data policies, their implementation and impact: A framework for comparison. *Government Information Quarterly, 31*(1), 17–29.
Zuiderwijk, A., & Janssen, M. (2014c). The negative effects of open government data-investigating the dark side of open data. In *Proceedings of the 15th Annual International Conference on Digital Government Research* (pp. 147–152). ACM.
Zuiderwijk, A., Janssen, M., & Dwivedi, Y. K. (2015). Acceptance and use predictors of open data technologies: Drawing upon the unified theory of acceptance and use of technology. *Government Information Quarterly, 32*(4), 429–440.
Zuiderwijk, A., Janssen, M., & Parnia, A. (2013, June). The complementarity of open data infrastructures: An analysis of functionalities. In *Proceedings of the 14th Annual International Conference on Digital Government Research* (pp. 166–171). ACM.
Zuiderwijk, A., Janssen, M., Choenni, S., Meijer, R., & Alibaks, R. S. (2012). Socio-technical Impediments of Open Data. *Electronic Journal of e-Government, 10*(2).

Chapter 2
Methodology of Research and Key Sources of Empirical Data

2.1 The Primary Reasons to Choose the Cases

One of the main reasons to choose Estonia and Kazakhstan as appropriate examples for cases study analysis is a unique context that each country could provide in a multitude of dimensions. In implementing technology-driven public sector reforms, these two nations resort to interesting and *sui generis* implementation strategies and tactics. Advancing various e-government and e-commerce platforms, each of the states demonstrates truly unique patterns in the development of open data projects such as a really active position of non-governmental players and local journalistic communities in the diffusion of open government philosophy in one country or a crucial role of independent networks of developers and business communities in another, and, at the same time, resorting to an extremely wide range of organizational, economic, and political tools and relying on different social platforms and technological projects. Furthermore, these countries demonstrate some differences in related administrative practices, too.

It is also necessary to note that both Estonia and partly Kazakhstan are well known for their e-government and e-participation solutions in public sector reforms, which could provide extremely favorable conditions to promote open data-driven philosophy. The phenomenon of digital government is often promoted by authorities in both countries not only as a tool of public sector innovations but also as a platform to boost public–private partnerships, especially in advancing communication and collaboration (Anthes, 2015; Björklund, 2016; Kalvet, 2007, 2012; Kassen, 2017a, b; Kitsing, 2008; Lember & Kalvet, 2014; Lember, Kattel & Tõnurist, 2018; Margetts & Naumann, 2017), which, however, tends to adopt different implementation strategies in adopting related technologies. Likewise, the role of central government in these nations varies significantly in advancing all e-government concepts, including in the open data area.

Another reason to choose these nations as appropriate examples to analyze the open data concept is a cultural and political context itself. Although sharing similar

M. Kassen, *Open Data Politics*, SpringerBriefs in Political Science,
https://doi.org/10.1007/978-3-030-11410-7_2

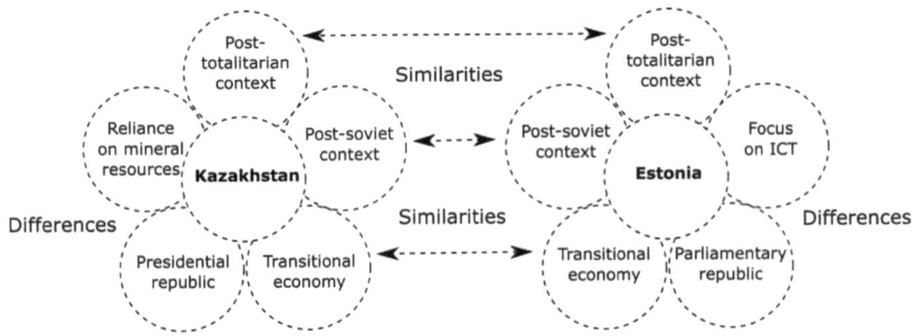

Fig. 2.1 Understanding country contexts in Kazakhstan and Estonia. *Source* Own illustration

socioeconomic features as, for example, a relatively small density of population and unitary system of governance, each of these two nations differs in other contexts. For instance, Estonia is globally famous for its adherence to main principles of social democracy, whereas Kazakhstan is a highly pro-capitalist republic. Each nation presents really interesting cases for the analysis of such new phenomena as open data politics. Due to a small size of public sector and transitional economies, they could be regarded as somewhat ideal experimental places to adopt various open government policies, demonstrating much-quicker reactions in advancing public sector reforms.

In this regard, the case of the open data movement in each of the regions itself could be characterized as atypical, unusual, and unique, the analysis of which, therefore, helps to understand better a multidimensional nature of the phenomena. Different institutional, political, administrative, economic, social, and technological backgrounds in each country really matter. For example, post-soviet Kazakhstan and, partly, Estonia share similar post-totalitarian contexts in a historic sense and are both often regarded as typical transitional nations. However, they differ in other more political and socioeconomic aspects of development. Kazakhstan is a strong presidential republic, which heavily relies on harnessing dividends from its mostly mineral resource-based economy. In this regard, Estonia is a parliamentary democracy, in which economy is mostly driven by innovations and processing industries (see Fig. 2.1).

2.2 The Methodology of the Research

Since the primary research question that shapes the study is the identification of key drivers, challenges, and stakeholders of open data phenomena as a presumably universal tool to boost public sector innovations, civic engagement, and e-participation, the whole case study research is based on the content analysis of various open data-driven start-ups and initiatives in both public and private sectors of economy equally in each country and policy review of key stakeholders' roles in open government politics there, namely public agencies who act as official providers of government datasets, independent developers who usually reuse the open data, for example, to create their own products and services, representatives of non-government and business sectors who often provide funding for the implementation of the projects, and finally journalists who propagate in mass media and social networks the public value of the concept.

2.2.1 The Overview of the Methodological Basis

Given that the research is mostly based on the analysis of empirical data from each of the two selected countries, the primary method of investigation is case study research with a combination of other related analytical tools such as context analysis of country backgrounds in political, economic, social, and international aspects, content analysis of official open government projects and independent open data-driven platforms, policy review of political communication channels between key stakeholders of the open data movement (e.g., government agents, representatives of various non-governmental organizations, independent developers, mass media, businesses, academia, etc.), and network analysis in order to understand how the concept is diffusing among policymakers and open data entrepreneurs in each country. The comparative analysis is helpful in comparing the results of the investigation with existing theories in the academic literature on the topic. Although the research includes the analysis of both quantitative and qualitative data, it is mostly qualitative.

2.2.2 The Overview of Key Tools of Analysis

The truly rapid and widespread diffusion of open government phenomena all over the world and, more importantly, an interesting trend in recent emergence of new promising open data-driven platforms to advance collaboration and participation among various stakeholders, both public and private ones, around the open data movement is ripe for close investigation and policy review through the investigation of actual cases. This was partly one of the reasons why the author of the book decided to resort to a cross-border case study research, which allows to observe closely a new phenomenon within its real-life context (Yin, 2013). In this regard, methodologically, the case study itself is based on a *scattergun approach*, applying in successive order the combination of three methods of research, namely context, policy, and content analysis. Consequently, this phenomenon is explored in each of these two nations through the prism of its key stakeholders, and identifying the main drivers and challenges of the open data movement with the primary goal of the whole investigation is to understand how this promising idea is developing, respectively, in an unusual context of emerging social democracy in Estonia and transitional post-totalitarian contexts of Kazakhstan. In this regard, the context analysis of country background is helpful in studying political and socioeconomic environments that are most conducive to the development of the concept and assessing the readiness of its key stakeholders to adopt and lead the open government movement in each of the nations.

The next research method, a policy review, is based on the results of semi-structured interviews with various stakeholders and close investigation of implementation and regulation strategies adopted by central governments, mostly at national levels in each country. In this regard, the research relies on the analysis of interesting patterns reflected in the emergence of new political trends in communication between key policymakers of the open data movement, which could help to shed light on the role of private and non-governmental sectors in the diffusion of the concept and reveal related networking activities among various non-traditional stakeholders, especially developers, journalists, non-governmental players, charities, academia, businesses, and technically savvy citizens. Finally, the content analysis of various open data-driven projects launched independently by members of civil society in each of the nations helps to understand better how the civic component of the open government paradigm is promoted. In general, the combination of these three methods is useful in understanding better political, social, and economic implications of country context on the development of the open data movement. Also, by analyzing challenges policymakers have to face every day in advancing related digital collaborative and participatory platforms, the author offers a number of practical recommendations on how to overcome them.

2.3 The Outline of the Main Stages of the Research

The case study itself, which is consistently repeated in a successive order in relationship to Estonia and Kazakhstan, includes five major stages such as the context analysis of the country background, i.e., the study of unique political and socioeconomic environments that are presumably conducive for the development of the open data concept in these two societies (*the first part*); the analysis of the freedom of information laws related to open data adopted by national authorities (*the second part*); the network analysis of how the open data concept is diffusing among its key stakeholders and technology entrepreneurs (*the third part*); the policy review of key trends in decision making in the area and analysis of how open data politics is promoted in various sectors of economy (*the fourth part*); and finally the content analysis of official open data platforms and independent open data-driven projects (*the fifth part*). The system analysis of generalizations and key findings on the open data movement received from multiple case studies is provided in the conclusion part (see Fig. 2.2).

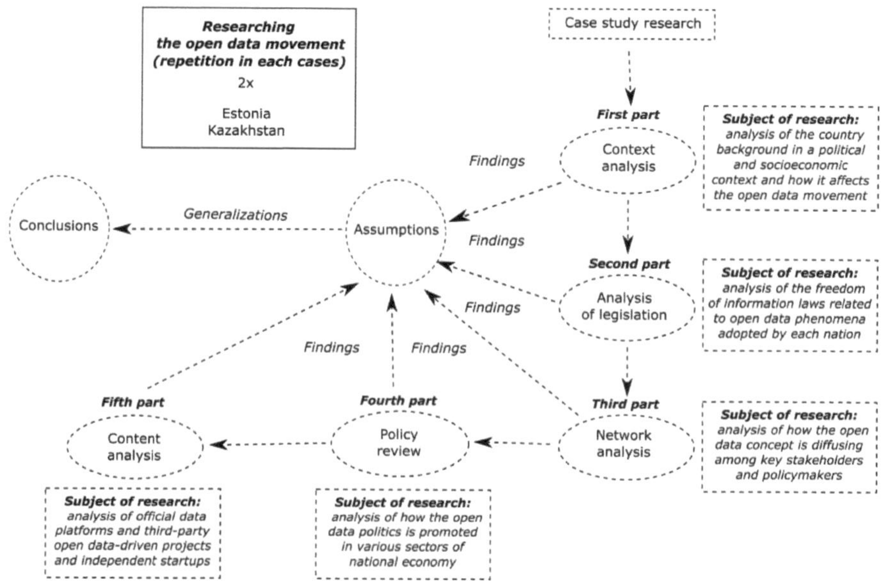

Fig. 2.2 Understanding key parts of case study research. *Source* Own illustration

2.3.1 The Context Analysis of the Country Background

The context analysis is really helpful in assessing the readiness of the two observed countries to adopt the open data-driven innovations in various areas, researching, first of all, the implications of domestic political, economic, social, and external international environments on the development of the open government concept as well as identifying key driving forces behind the mere desire to promote open data as a tool to build a cost-effective public administration ecosystem. Another goal of the context analysis is to shed light on potential challenges in advancing the concept related to the different cultural contexts of examined nations so that to compare them with the results of the content analysis in the following parts of the research. In this respect, various country contexts are studied such as *political environment*, which helps to analyze the influence of established political institutions and traditions of decision making on the development of the open data movement (the first stage of the analysis); *economic environment*, where analysis is crucial in measuring the infrastructural readiness of the nations to adopt various open data-driven technologies (the second stage); *social environment*, which is extremely useful in understanding the cultural contexts in given societies, e.g., in analyzing the public mind-set of citizenry, the popularity of traditions of civic engagement, collaboration and participation in local communities, self-governance, fundraising activities, participation of non-governmental organizations, etc. (*the third stage*), and *international environment*, which is helpful in studying the effects of international cooperation between various stakeholders both public and private, image-making activities of national authorities, foreign investment, funding, consultations by international organizations in the area, etc. (*the fourth stage*).

2.3.2 The Legal Analysis of Open Data Legislation

The analysis of regulatory basis related to the promotion of official, semi-official, and independent open data-driven projects in government is important in understanding implementation policies in the area, especially in terms of legal opportunities that are conducive to public reuse of government datasets. Traditionally, the legislation related to freedom of information provides a primary legal platform to advance the concept both politically and organizationally, making the process of the open data publication more regulated and systematic. Additionally, the emergence of new legal instruments to regulate the area such as public sector information ordinances and administrative directives adopted at regional, i.e., pan-European instances (Janssen, 2011), e.g., in case of Estonia, as well as national and local levels of governance in both countries is indicative of the increasing trend toward the diversification of related regulatory mechanisms in the area. Reflecting the new trend in e-government and latest practices in promoting open data-driven projects, these new instruments of regulation allow to apply more adaptive legislation in the area, making the process of the concept adoption more interactive and cost-effective.

2.3.3 The Network Analysis of the Relationship Between Key Stakeholders of the Open Data Movement

The main purpose of network analysis is to understand how the concept of open data is diffusing among its stakeholders by identifying the invisible communication channels and networking chains that presumably emerge in the processes, especially in analyzing political interactions between key players in the e-government area (Khan & Park, 2013), i.e., public agents, developers, policy entrepreneurs from local business and non-governmental sectors, journalists, academia, etc. In this regard, the analysis of social relationships and the results of semi-structured interviews with them is one of the most important steps in this study, taking into account the empirical character of the whole research. In this respect, the analysis of professional ties and communication links related to the topic, in particular to the key nodes, i.e., actors in such open data-driven interactions, is helpful in identifying the key areas of cooperation, the closeness of the nodes and groups of open data entrepreneurs, the main groups of interests and associated lobbying activities, and other properties of professional communication in the area.

2.3.4 *The Policy Review of Official Open Data Strategies and Government Initiatives*

As one of the most important steps in conducting the case study, the policy review of the open data strategies and government initiatives both at national and local levels helps to identify the strong and weak points in implementation policies in the area. In addition, the analysis of how government agencies distribute public information and datasets through official portals, especially from cross-institutional perspectives (Altayar, 2018; Baack, 2015; Chatfield & Reddick, 2017; Kassen, 2018c; Pinto, Bernardini & Viterbo, 2018; Sayogo, Pardo & Cook, 2014; Wang & Lo, 2016), could help to understand better the overall organization of the work in the area, which often reflects the established approaches to the idea of open government as a political concept (Lourenço, 2015) and indicates to the potential challenges in their operation. The availability of such tools as registration, personalization and categorization of open data, filtering algorithms, visitation statistics, advanced search engines, various language versions and even opportunities to publish own open data by business entities, private corporations, non-governmental organizations and individuals are crucial indicators in assessing the overall readiness of the public sector to adopt the open data concept at different organizational and bureaucratic levels. Likewise, the publication of government datasets in various digital formats and platforms and the availability of downloadable training handbooks and guides for potential developers and technically savvy citizens help to evaluate the technological readiness of the platforms. These networking platforms should be tailored to the needs of citizens and specifics of business activities at local levels. The operations are usually conducted by those who call themselves technology entrepreneurs and developers, i.e., those who represent the middleman chain in the open data-driven realization philosophy. One more aspect of policy review is the evaluation of public relations tools embedded into the platforms, especially in analyzing the impact of such instruments of publicity as, for example, news alerts, tweets, various forums, and civic comments. These instruments could boost communication not only with the public but also with local media communities which are beginning to play an increasingly important role in diffusing promising data-driven journalism (Appelgren & Nygren, 2014).

2.3.5 *The Content Analysis of Independent Open Data-Driven Projects*

The next important stage of the study is the content analysis of third-party open data-driven projects itself, which activity and popularity are indicatives of the overall success in propagating the concept of open government among those who are supposed to reuse the datasets. After all, it is the reuse of government datasets by members of civil society that constitutes the core of open data philosophy.

Therefore, the evaluation of independent civic data-driven projects in the e-government area could be helpful in understanding key trends in the development of the phenomena in each country. Moreover, taking into account the fact that government is now beginning to play a role of only a datasets provider, which itself is presented as a raw material and acting therefore as an ideological platform to further the open government movement among developers, journalists, businesspersons and other important stakeholders rather than just a traditional focal point of all government services and decision making, the promotion of independent open data-driven projects is a key benchmark of analysis. In this respect, it is important to understand the invisible mechanism of open data politics since the official public policies in the area, which usually include such components as regulation, publication of datasets and socioeconomic incentives that government sends to other stakeholders, is just one important but not that crucial part of the whole open data-driven realm. It is merely a tip of the iceberg (see Fig. 2.3).

In this regard, the research focuses on studying open data-driven civic engagement and related networking projects that promote political communication, collaboration, and participation in each country. The results of field studies conducted during early stages of the research in 2015–2017, the document analysis of

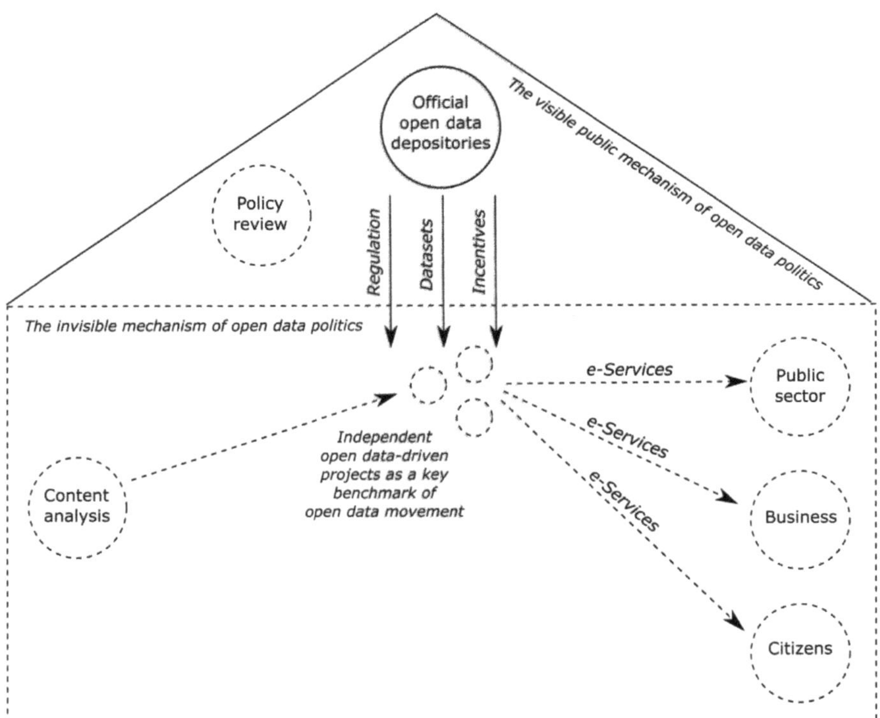

Fig. 2.3 The review of open data-driven projects as a key benchmark of content analysis. *Source* Own illustration

such data as official strategies, laws, speeches, etc. as well as content analysis of public and private open data portals, and, more importantly, independent third-party open data-driven projects and start-ups and social media statistics help to identify the most popular civic engagement initiatives in the area. In this regard, such online tools of statistical analysis as the Google Trend, Social Bakers, and others were useful in studying the general trends in the development of the open data movement and measuring popularity of particular data-driven projects and related social media platforms in each of these two studied nations.

2.3.6 The Comparative and System Analysis of the Open Data Movement: Locating Typical Drivers and Challenges

One of the most important steps in this case study research is a comparative and system analysis of key findings from each country that is presented in the conclusion chapter of the book in an attempt to locate distinctive trends in the development of the open data movement as a platform to boost civic engagement, public sector innovations, economic development and even political reforms. Another goal of the analysis is to provide perspectives on typical drivers and challenges in adopting the concept derived from the context of real cases and administrative practices. Additionally, the analysis of similarities and differences of the open data movement in each country is helpful in understanding the implications of local cultural contexts, i.e., political, economic, social and other environments on the development of the phenomena and in generating a number of practical recommendations for policymakers and practitioners in the area.

2.4 Identifying Key Sources of Empirical Data for Case Study Research

This paragraph is dedicated to the identification and systematization of key sources of empirical data and statistical information on the development of open data movement in each country, which was necessary to collect and analyze in order to support key arguments and findings of the research. The study is mostly based on the analysis of the results of semi-structured interviews with various open data players and intensive field studies in Estonia and Kazakhstan in 2015–2017 as well as document and content analysis of sources from various government bodies, international organizations and statistical agencies. In this regard, the data is investigated from the following perspectives:

(1) *the analysis of related regulatory acts*, which are also subdivided in the research, for example, in accordance with a principle of administrative division (e.g., open data legislation at regional, national, and local levels of public administration and governance) and with relevance to the promotion of open government phenomena (e.g., direct and indirect influence on the area, associated e-government laws, freedom of information acts, various public sector ordinances, directives and memorandums, etc.);
(2) *the analysis of key sources of official data and statistics*, which are then subdivided in accordance with, for example, a geographic principle (e.g., statistics at global, national and local levels of the open data movement) and with an authority of the source (e.g., official datasets, i.e., published by government itself, and unofficial datasets, which are usually provided by, for example, non-governmental organizations, universities, private telecommunication corporations, think tanks, citizens themselves, etc.);
(3) *the analysis of various open government portals and open data-driven projects*, which, in turn, are subdivided in the investigation in accordance with the type of platforms (e.g., ordinary desktop and mobile versions of the portals); in accordance with the type of digital services (e.g., platforms that provide either information, interactive or transactional e-services); in accordance with the target audiences (e.g., peer-to-peer platforms designed for either citizens, businesses or developers) and in accordance with the authority of open data platforms (e.g., projects created either directly by government or autonomously by such players as non-governmental organizations, independent developers, technically savvy citizens, businesses, etc.);
(4) *the analysis of other sources of data and information* (e.g., mass media, statistics from online search machines, web-counters, official accounts in social media, etc.).

2.4.1 The Analysis of Regulatory Acts

The analysis of legal acts that directly regulate various aspects of the open data movement, transparency of government and freedom of information as one of the key sources of relevant official information on the topic is extremely helpful in this research, especially in understanding official implementation policies adopted by government stakeholders in each country. The analysis of open government laws is also useful in understanding the historical milestones of related public sector reforms. Moreover, taking into account a top-down structure of public administration and unambiguous overwhelming influence of national authorities in these two unitary states in adopting any administrative acts, the analysis of laws and related public documents such as e-government directives is helpful also in understanding the role of the public sector itself in advancing the idea of open government data. The fact that there are official open digital repositories available online that allow viewing almost any laws and legal acts in the area in each country, often in chronological order, significantly simplifies the task. In this regard, the regulatory acts are analyzed in accordance with their force, type, and direct or indirect relevance to the topic such as national and local laws, state programs, national strategies, directives, charters, ordinances, etc. Many regulatory acts are often provided in English, which serves as *lingua franca* in e-government-related communication among professionals in the area, dramatically broadening an available pool of related documents for the study. In general, the analysis of open government laws is subdivided in accordance with the following structure of legislation:

I. *On an administrative principle*:

(a) Regional legislation (e.g., in case of Estonia, legal acts adopted by the European Commission and its diverse agencies and associated intergovernmental bodies in the area, pan-European action plans, directives, memorandums, development programs, strategies, etc.);
(b) National legislation (e.g., national laws, strategies, programs and implementation plans, presidential and central government directives and resolutions, ministerial orders, etc.);
(c) Local legislation (local government directives and city ordinances, implementation plans and programs, charters of public–private partnerships in the area, etc.).

II. *On a relevance to the topic*:

(a) Direct, i.e., focused specifically on open data regulation (e.g., freedom of information laws, public information acts, open government memorandums, etc.);
(b) Indirect, i.e., focused generally on regulation in related technology-driven public sector reforms (e.g., informatization laws, e-government directives, information security acts, etc.).

III. *Key regulation documents*:

In Estonia:

1. The Public Information Act (2000).
2. The Information Society Services Act (2004).
3. The Estonian Information Society Strategy (2013).

In Kazakhstan:

1. The Law on Access to Information (2015).
2. The informatization law (2007).
3. The strategy—Information Kazakhstan-2020 (2013).

2.4.2 *The Analysis of Key Sources of Official Data and Statistics*

The analysis of key sources of official data and statistics is important in understanding the main stakeholders and key trends of the open data movement in various areas such as public administration, politics, economy, ICT-sector, transportation, regional development, and even foreign policy in each country. Such statistical information, provided both on a chronological and geographic order, as the number of published datasets, the popularity of certain open data-driven services, the volume and type of provided transactions, the size of annual budget assignations allocated for the implementation of the open data projects, the speed of transactions, the number of registered users, the number of the launched open government projects, the level of the Internet penetration, the level of digital divide, etc. is definitely helpful in analyzing the topic from various socioeconomic and technological perspectives. In this regard, there are a lot of reputable official government bodies and independent non-governmental and non-commercial organizations which provide a wide range of statistical data such as national statistical agencies, the international intergovernmental organizations and watchdogs, research centers and think tanks, universities and ICT-associations both at regional, national, and global levels that provide various data relevant to the topic.

The globalization of digital government agendas and promotion of cross-border open government, open data, e-government, and e-participation networking platforms allows to easily monitor, assess, and even promote more universal and standardized mechanisms of technology-driven reforms and enablers of public sector invitations in the area in an intrinsically international manner (Kassen, 2014). For example, such organizations as the Open Data Barometer, the Open Knowledge Foundation, national statistical agencies of, respectively, Estonia and Kazakhstan, the United Nations Public Administration Network (UNPAN), the World Bank, the Open Government Partnership, the European Statistical Agency (Eurostat), the Asian Bank of Reconstruction and Development, the International Human Rights Watch, the Transparency International, Microsoft, Google and IBM corporations all provide statistical data that monitor at least some aspects of the open government development in each country. In this respect, the categories of statistical information are subdivided in accordance with the geographical principle and authority of the source:

I. *On a geographical principle*:

(a) Global (e.g., international intergovernmental institutions, global non-governmental organizations, watchdogs, research centers, telecommunication corporations, etc.);
(b) National (e.g., governmental statistical agencies, national non-governmental organizations, universities, think tanks, etc.);
(c) Local (e.g., local governmental agencies, non-governmental organizations, communities of developers and journalists, etc.).

II. *On the authority of source*:

(a) Government (e.g., national governmental agencies such as agencies of statistics and their subsidiaries at local levels, presidential administrations, offices of prime ministers, various ministries, etc. in each country);
(b) Independent (e.g., international and domestic intergovernmental organizations such as the United Nations, the World Bank, the Open Government Partnership, local non-governmental organizations, universities, research centers, and media).

III. *Key sources of official data and statistics*:

(A) *In Estonia*:

Government sources:

1. The Statistical Agency of Estonia. https://www.stat.ee
2. The Estonian Information System Authority. https://www.ria.ee/en/
3. The Ministry of Economic Affairs and Communications. https://www.mkm.ee/en.

Independent sources:

1. The Open Estonia Foundation Project. http://oef.org.ee/en
2. The National Foundation of Civil Society. www.kysk.ee/eng
3. The e-Government Academy. http://www.ega.ee/
4. The Network of Estonian Nonprofit Organizations. http://www.ngo.ee/neno
5. The Estonian Village Movement. http://kodukant.kovtp.ee/.

(B) *In Kazakhstan*:

Government sources:

1. The Kazakh Agency of Statistics. http://www.stat.gov.kz;
2. The Ministry of Investments and Development of Kazakhstan. http://www.mid.gov.kz
3. The National Agency for Technological Development. http://natd.gov.kz
4. The Kazakh National Infocommunication Holding. www.zerde.gov.kz/en/kholding.htm.

Independent sources:

1. The National Information Technologies Agency. www.nitec.kz
2. The Infocommunication Development Fund of Kazakhstan. www.ictfund.kz
3. Kazinform Information Agency. http://www.inform.kz
4. The Legal Policy Research Centre. http://lprc.kz/en.

(C) *Global sources of data and statistics*:

1. The Open Data Barometer. http://opendatabarometer.org
2. The Global Open Data Index. http://index.okfn.org
3. The United Nations Public Administration Network (UNPAN)—http://www.unpan.org (especially, the UNPAN E-Government Surveys—2003, 2004, 2005, 2008, 2010, 2012, 2014, 2016, 2018 which allow to track the progress in the area in each country in chronological order);
4. The Organization for Economic Cooperation and Development. Government at a Glance 2015. https://www.oecd.org/gov
5. The Open Government Partnership. http://www.opengovpartnership.org
6. The World Justice Project. http://data.worldjusticeproject.org/opengov/
7. The Open Knowledge Foundation. https://okfn.org/about/
8. The Open Data 500 Global Network. http://www.opendata500.com/
9. The European Agency of Statistics. http://ec.europa.eu/eurostat
10. The European Regional Development Fund. http://ec.europa.eu/regional_policy/en/funding/erdf/
11. The Doing Business Rating. http://www.doingbusiness.org
12. The International Telecommunication Union. http://www.itu.int.

2.4.3 The Analyses of Open Government Portals and Open Data-Driven Platforms

The content analysis of national open government portals and data platforms is the most important part of the case study research as it helps to understand the strategic execution of the concept, in general, and implementation tactics of open data-driven public sector reforms, in particular, consistently in a number of public agencies and in a successive manner in each of the observed nations. Such information as the type of government platforms and their subdivision into the desktop and mobile versions, dataset platforms designed for operating systems (e.g., Windows Mobile, Android, and Apple iOS); the algorithms and mechanisms of operation, the presence and type of the user identification in such systems; the type of services (e.g., informational, interactive and transactional, paid e-services, etc.); target audiences (e.g., e-services for citizens and businesses or exclusively for developers); peer-to-peer and civic engagement projects and other information is useful in analyzing strong and weak points of open data implementation mechanisms from different technological points of view. In analyzing such information, it is also necessary to understand the implications of socioeconomic and, more importantly, political character in the development of the phenomena. In general, the analysis of official and various independent open data-driven projects helps to identify the role of main stakeholders in the development of the movement and understand better the whole invisible mechanism and all internal chains of open data politics. In this regard, the information is investigated in accordance with different institutional levels at which open data platforms are promoted and also technological types of open data-driven start-ups and related networking projects, which were independently created and initiated by citizens themselves:

I. *Institutional levels of government data platforms*:

  (a) Regional data platforms (e.g., open government data platforms promoted at regional levels);
  (b) National data platforms (e.g., open government data platforms promoted at national levels);
  (c) Local data platforms (e.g., open government data platforms promoted at local levels).

II. *Technological types of open-driven platforms and projects*:

  (a) Networking platforms (e.g., the platforms, which are created by a community of independent developers to promote open data-driven networking and collaboration);
  (b) Independent open data-driven platforms (e.g., various open data-driven platforms and applications created for citizens, business, non-governmental organizations, and mass media such as public relations, educational, peer-to-peer initiatives, and start-ups).

III. *Key empirical cases*:

(A) *In Estonia*:

The key national open data platform:

1. The Open Data Portal of Estonia. https://opendata.riik.ee/

The key networking platforms:

1. The Garage48 Project. http://garage48.org/
2. The Open Estonia Foundation Project. http://oef.org.ee/en/about-us/
3. Tehnopol. The technological business incubator of Estonia. http://www.tehnopol.ee

The key independent open data-driven platforms:

1. The Meieraha project. http://meieraha.eu/?lang=en
2. The Valitsemise Valvurid project. http://valvurid.err.ee
3. The Riigiraha project. http://riigiraha.fin.ee.

(D) *In Kazakhstan*:

The key national open data platforms:

1. The Open Data Project of Kazakhstan. http://data.egov.kz/
2. The open government project of Kazakhstan—http://open.egov.kz.

The key networking platforms:

1. The Tech Garden Project. http://techgarden.kz/
2. The HackDay Kazakhstan Project. http://hackday2015.kz/
3. The Tedxastana Project. http://tedxastana.com.

The key independent open data-driven platforms:

1. The Healthcare project. https://itunes.apple.com/us/app/zdorov-e+-medicinskij-spravocnik/id1133507478
2. The Business registration checker. http://databay.kz/legal-entity
3. The TengeApp project. http://tengeapp.kz.

(E) *In Europe* (*the pan-European open data platforms*):

1. The Open Data Europe Project. https://open-data.europa.eu
2. The European Open Data portal. http://europeandataportal.eu
3. The European Public Sector Information Platform. http://www.epsiplatform.eu
4. The public open data project. http://publicdata.eu.

(D) *In the United States* (*for comparative cross-institutional analysis*):

1. The open data platform at the national level (The U.S. Federal Government). http://data.gov
2. The open data platform at the provincial level (The State of Illinois). http://data.illinois.gov
3. The open data platform at the local level (The Cook County). http://data.cookcounty.gov
4. The open data platform at the urban level (The City of Chicago). http://data.cityofchicago.org.

2.4.4 Additional Sources of Data

The analysis of data and information available from such additional sources as mass media (e.g., national and local printing and electronic mass media), online statistical tools (e.g., web-counters, Google Trend, Social Bakers, etc.), official accounts in social networking platforms (e.g., in Twitter, Facebook, Instagram, VKontakte, Google Plus, Github, Bitbucket, Sourceforge, etc.) is helpful, too, especially in investigating such aspects of the open data movement in each of the nations as, for example, the official public awareness strategies of government agencies in the area, visitation to the open government portals and other public e-government Web sites, the communication activity of government officials and ministers with citizens, businesses, media and peers, the popularity of certain types of open data-driven services, projects and initiatives, networking activity between main stakeholders, etc.

References

Altayar, M. S. (2018). Motivations for open data adoption: An institutional theory perspective. *Government Information Quarterly*.

Anthes, G. (2015). Estonia: A model for e-government. *Communications of the ACM, 58*(6), 18–20.

Appelgren, E., & Nygren, G. (2014). Data Journalism in Sweden: Introducing new methods and genres of journalism into "old" organizations. *Digital Journalism, 2*(3), 394–405.

Baack, S. (2015). Datafication and empowerment: How the open data movement re-articulates notions of democracy, participation, and journalism. *Big Data & Society, 2*(2), 2053951715594634.

Björklund, F. (2016). E-government and moral citizenship: The case of Estonia. *Citizenship Studies, 20*(6–7), 914–931.

Chatfield, A. T., & Reddick, C. G. (2017). A longitudinal cross-sector analysis of open data portal service capability: The case of Australian local governments. *Government Information Quarterly, 34*(2), 231–243.

Janssen, K. (2011). The influence of the PSI directive on open government data: An overview of recent developments. *Government Information Quarterly, 28*(4), 446–456.

Kalvet, T. (2007). *The Estonian information society developments since the 1990s*. PRAXIS.

Kalvet, T. (2012). Innovation: A factor explaining e-government success in Estonia. *Electronic Government, An International Journal, 9*(2), 142–157.

Kassen, M. (2014). Globalization of e-government: Open government as a global agenda; benefits, limitations and ways forward. *Information Development, 30*(1), 51–58.

Kassen, M. (2017a). Open data in Kazakhstan: Incentives, implementation and challenges. *Information Technology & People, 30*(2), 301–323.

Kassen, M. (2017b). Open data and e-government–related or competing ecosystems: A paradox of open government and promise of civic engagement in Estonia. *Information Technology for Development*, 1–27.

Kassen, M. (2018). Adopting and managing open data: Stakeholder perspectives, challenges and policy recommendations. *Aslib Journal of Information Management, 70*(5), 518–537.

Khan, G. F., & Park, H. W. (2013). The e-government research domain: A triple helix network analysis of collaboration at the regional, country, and institutional levels. *Government Information Quarterly, 30*(2), 182–193.

Kitsing, M. (2008, May). Explaining the e-government success in Estonia. In *Proceedings of the 2008 International Conference on Digital Government Research* (pp. 429–430). Digital Government Society of North America.

Lember, V., & Kalvet, T. (2014). Estonia. In *Public procurement, innovation and policy* (pp. 127–149). Berlin, Heidelberg: Springer.

Lember, V., Kattel, R., & Tõnurist, P. (2018). Technological capacity in the public sector: The case of Estonia. *International Review of Administrative Sciences, 84*(2), 214–230.

Lourenço, R. P. (2015). An analysis of open government portals: A perspective of transparency for accountability. *Government Information Quarterly, 32*(3), 323–332.

Margetts, H., & Naumann, A. (2017). Government as a platform: What can Estonia show the world. Research paper, University of Oxford.

Pinto, H. D. S., Bernardini, F., & Viterbo, J. (2018, May). How cities categorize datasets in their open data portals: an exploratory analysis. In *Proceedings of the 19th Annual International Conference on Digital Government Research: Governance in the Data Age* (p. 25). ACM.

Sayogo, D. S., Pardo, T. A., & Cook, M. (2014, January). A framework for benchmarking open government data efforts. In *2014 47th Hawaii International Conference on System Sciences (HICSS)* (pp. 1896–1905). IEEE.

Wang, H. J., & Lo, J. (2016). Adoption of open government data among government agencies. *Government Information Quarterly, 33*(1), 80–88.

Yin, R. K. (2013). *Case study research: Design and methods*. Sage publications.

Chapter 3
Open Data Politics in Estonia: Advancing Open Government in the Context of Ubiquitous Digital State

3.1 Introduction: Setting the Research Agenda

A Nordic nation that reestablished its independence in 1991 and almost graduated from being a transitional economy, Estonia is globally well known today as one of the pioneers in promoting innovative public sector reforms and digital solutions in government technology, especially in creating very sophisticated public administration ecosystems or harnessing a cost-effective potential of electronic banking. One more public sector innovation where this country is leading in a global sense is the development of Internet voting (Drechsler & Madise, 2004; Krimmer, Triessnig, & Volkamer, 2007; Madise & Priit, 2011; Vinkel & Krimmer, 2016). Moreover, the intrinsic focus on measures that are specifically aimed to ensure better transparency of various government institutions helps this nation to step on the ultimate destination of any technology-driven reforms in public administration, which is *e-democracy*, slowly but surely transferring e-government agendas into a political dimension of discussion.

Interestingly enough, steadily demonstrating impressive results in advancing various technology-driven platforms such as e-governance, e-participation, e-commerce, e-voting, e-taxation, and many other e-initiatives, this country is closely associated today all over the world with a brand name that it should be proud of—electronic or e-Estonia (Liiv, 2017; Schnurer, 2015). Being a birthplace of a plethora of various initially small technological start-ups and projects such as Skype, TransferWise, and GrabCAD among others that later gained an extremely widespread popularity and global market success, Estonia is an ideal testing ground to observe a dynamic nature of open data politics in all its diversity in one particular isolated case.

In this regard, the chapter analyzes the development of open data phenomena in an unusual context of a country that is universally well known today as one of the global leaders in promoting information society, especially demonstrating impressive advances in building sophisticated e-government, e-commerce, e-voting and

M. Kassen, *Open Data Politics*, SpringerBriefs in Political Science,
https://doi.org/10.1007/978-3-030-11410-7_3

recently also blockchain governance ecosystems. Paying special attention to the investigation of main implementation and regulation policies, stakeholders and challenges of the open data movement in Estonia, the author of the book argues that the presence of established democratic institutions and civil society as well as an incredibly developed and dynamic software industry that values open business competition and professional curiosity along with a strong sense of patriotism and adherence to a particular neighborhood deeply rooted in Estonian society has played a crucial role in the diffusion of the concept. In general, open data turns out to be a truly complex multidimensional phenomenon that for its full implementation requires collaborative efforts from all stakeholders both public and private.

3.2 The Country Context Analysis: Understanding Socioeconomic and Political Environments

3.2.1 The Economic Environment: The Promise of Public Sector Innovations

The reuse of open data in civic and private sectors could promise certain economic dividends, first of all, in boosting civic engagement and business activity at local levels. In this regard, the economic incentive is probably a number one motivation for Estonia, a homeland of a slightly more than one million people, to harness a promising potential of the phenomena to boost public sector innovations in the area and all other aspects of the country context in both political and social domains are indirectly interconnected with the economic one. The lack of vast reserves in mineral resources and natural wealth is regarded as a key factor (Anthes, 2015) that explains an extreme desire of this small nation to develop a knowledge economy that would rely mostly on innovations and advanced technologies in generating national capital. Whether it is in food industry, agriculture or telecommunications, Estonians always try to resort to the latest technological developments in those fields in order to make production cost-efficient and, more importantly, sustainable in such a compact market. The widespread use of open source software solutions in various sectors of economy and an intrinsic focus on those industries where this country has a definitive competitive advantage, first of all, in smart technologies and logistics, helped this nation to advance both economically and technologically.

As a nationwide strategy of development, this really pragmatic economic policy as arguably the only way to survive and prosper has proved to be very effective and prudent. This allowed Estonia to relatively quickly graduate from its mostly transitional status (Drechsler, 1995) after almost two decades of quite an intensive work, building new economy, basically, from the scratch. In this regard, even the active promotion of technology-driven public sector reforms started in the 1990s has been dictated by the conditions of the tough economic reality at that time, which required not only more effective but also less expensive solutions in public administration by resorting to a promise of digitalization in various areas of human activity (Åström, Jonsson, Hinsberg, & Karlsson, 2013; Kalvet, 2012; Kirillov, Shmorgun, & Lamas, 2011; Kitsing, 2011; Lember, Kattel & Tõnurist, 2018; McBride, Matheus, Toots, Kalvet, & Krimmer, 2018; Nielsen, 2017; Peedu & Lamas, 2011).

The digitalization has become a watchword of almost all public sector reforms in Estonia. An impressive progress in advancing various e-government, e-participation, and especially, e-voting and e-banking platforms is a real exemplar of the successful path that this nation has chosen to embrace. The combination of economic policies aimed at propagating the public value of knowledge economy and the fact that it has a relatively small size of public sector, which, to a greater extent, should be regarded as one more competitive advantage, helped Estonia to build quickly a well-functioning digital state. The emergence of the open data concept that is gaining ever-growing popularity all over the country today could provide a new platform to boost national economy in a digital manner even further. According to the European Commission, the reuse of open data could potentially generate billions of Euros every year (Information Age, 2011), provided that all member states of the European Union would develop an economic ecosystem that encourages technological innovations in the area.

In this respect, Estonia has all economic preconditions to prosper in this direction, especially in advancing open data-driven platforms to render new electronic services as a presumably cost-effective addition to its excellent traditional top-down digital government platforms. Ideally, by publishing various datasets through the official depositary, the public sector could potentially gain certain benefits from its reuse in third-party open data-driven projects, reflected, for example, in the creation of not only new digital products for private sector, which already receives an extensively wide range of digital services through national e-government systems, but also in the generation of cost-effective open data-driven public sector innovations for government itself since it could create a new channel for communication and more intensive interactive networking with citizens (see Fig. 3.1).

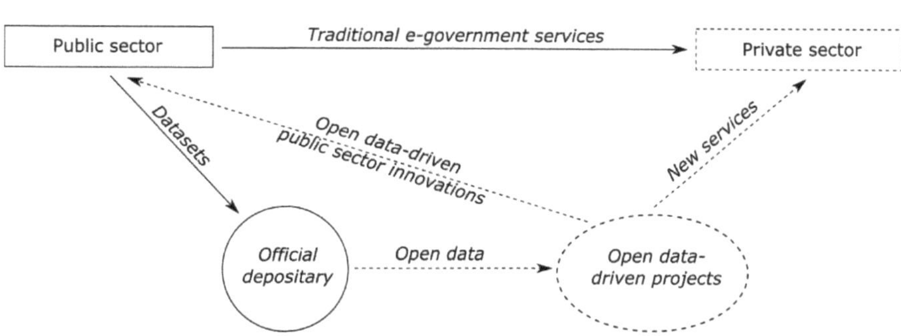

Fig. 3.1 The cost-effective mechanism of open data-driven public sector innovations in Estonia. *Source* Own illustration

3.2.2 The Social Environment: The Promise of Civic Engagement and Collaboration

First of all, it is necessary to emphasize that private-partnerships and inter-institutional cooperation play a crucial role in advancing digital agendas in Estonia, especially in advancing such a sophisticated and highly interconnected mechanism of data exchange in both e-commerce and e-government platforms as an X-road ecosystem (Anthes, 2015; Pappel, Pappel, Tepandi, & Draheim, 2017; Paide, Pappel, Vainsalu, & Draheim, 2018). In this respect, analyzing the fundamental factors that could explain a truly rapid advance of technology-driven reforms, Kitsing (2008) from Estonian Business School pointed that the formula of success in building digital state in this country is possible due to close collaboration between both public and private sectors of economy, especially in transforming cardinally the institutional foundations of existing e-government and e-commerce ecosystems. Such an intrinsic focus on public–private partnership in developing related digital platforms in government is rarely seen today in the world, taking into account the fact that such projects are usually introduced and implemented mostly by public agencies themselves in a really top-down manner (Abu-Shanab & Bataineh, 2014; Bakunzibake, Grönlund, & Klein, 2016; Chen & Huang, 2015; Chen, A. J., Pan, S. L., Zhang, Huang, & Zhu, 2009; Gao & Lee, 2017; Hui & Hayllar, 2010; Klischewski, 2003; Layne & Lee, 2001; Linders, 2012; Moon & Welch, 2005).

One of the reasons for such collaborative policy is again related to a pragmatic approach adopted by Estonian authorities in an attempt to create more interactive, open and, more importantly, cost-effective ecosystem for all stakeholders. Feedback and customization have always been welcomed from everyone who operates in Estonian e-government and e-commerce platforms, leading to greater participation and engagement. This sui generis socioeconomic context allows to presume that active stance of private and civic sectors could be helpful to develop open data-driven projects, too. The reuse of government datasets usually requires readiness of local developers, entrepreneurs, and technologically savvy citizens to embrace the new phenomenon as a promising platform to launch various independent civic engagement projects and business start-ups. In this regard, the social environment reflected in the traditionally strong stance of civil society in public sector reforms in Estonia could be really conducive to the popularization of open data philosophy among various groups of local developers and civic communities, though mostly in urban neighborhoods.

Furthermore, such socioeconomic challenges associated with the sustainable development of digital governance as digital divide (Ebbers Jansen & van Deursen, 2016; Helbig, Gil-García, & Ferro, 2009; Polat, 2012) and lack of infrastructure (Basu, 2004; Dada, 2006) are settled much easier in high-income countries (UNPAN, 2018), all the more so if they are compact economies, e.g., Singapore, Bahrain or United Arab Emirates (Ahmad & Khalid, 2017; Baum & Mahizhnan, 2015; Meftah, Gharleghi, & Samadi, 2015). Therefore, one more important aspect of successful advance of open government platforms is related to the socioeconomic

Table 3.1 The Internet penetration in Estonia in 2009–2016

Year	Internet users	Penetration (% of total population) (%)	Total population	Non-users (Internetless)
2016	1,196,521	91.40	1,309,104	112,583
2015	1,170,726	89.20	1,312,558	141,832
2014	1,108,769	84.20	1,316,203	207,434
2013	1,048,120	79.40	1,320,050	271,930
2012	1,037,914	78.40	1,324,040	286,126
2011	1,015,972	76.50	1,328,068	312,096
2010	987,078	74.10	1,332,089	345,011
2009	968,609	72.50	1,336,013	367,404

Source Elaboration based on sample data from Internet Live Stats (2017a)

readiness of local communities to adopt new technologies. In this regard, with a population of approximately 1.3 million people, Estonia is one of the least populous nations in the European Union. However, it enjoys a soaring level of the Internet penetration (see Table 3.1) and widespread use of smart technologies in households (Kalja, Põld, Robal, & Vallner, 2011; Kamińska-Korolczuk & Kijewska, 2017).

One more feature, which one can observe in local labor market, is increasing popularity of ICT education and professions among youth. This trend is partly caused by narrow specialization of local economy (Kalvet, 2004), which relies heavily on revenues from various innovative start-ups and technological platforms and demands specialists in related areas, especially in software industries. This is one of the reasons why an increasing number of young Estonians prefer to choose computer science and other non-humanitarian professions as their major in local universities. For example, twice as many students pursue ICT careers in Estonia than the average in other OECD countries (e-Estonia, 2018). Moreover, computer programming is a highly popular course in many local schools and regarded by many pupils as one of the most interesting pastimes. In this respect, such environment of collaborative learning is also actively supported by authorities, especially by organizing various hobby groups in middle and high schools (University of Tartu, 2015).

It is also interesting to note that the local education system itself is highly digitalized. The Estonian Education Information System (EHIS), a state database platform that integrates all information related to education, stores details about all local education institutions, teachers, students, graduation documents, study materials and curricula (e-Estonia, 2018). In this regard, such interactive platforms in the education sphere as e-School (digital school management ecosystem for administrators, teachers, students, and their parents), e-Schoolbag (interactive electronic textbook database for students), OPIQ (cost-effective nationwide centralized database of certified teaching and learning materials), Foxcademy (interactive science studies database for middle and high schools), Roboversity (pre-university robotics education platform), and ELIIS (pre-schools and kindergartens education and management ecosystem) generate an extremely big amount of data for public consumption. All schools are connected to these innovative solutions. As a result, all graduates of Estonian schools are prepared to live in a digital environment in various areas of human activity and could continue their education in ICT majors in universities and colleges if they wish to become professionals in those areas.

In this regard, the Tallinn University of Technology (TUT), University of Tartu and the Estonian Information Technology College (EITC) are well known as three key education venues that prepare a lion's share of computer specialists in this country. This is one of the reasons why the Tehnopol Park, a globally renowned technological incubator, which is situated near the TUT, provides a basement for more than 200 Estonian software and telecommunication companies, among which one could find a technological headquarter of such universally well-known enterprise as Skype (Tehnopol, 2018). The Tehnopol or, as it is often referred to, *Tallinn Science Park* (Varblane & Varblane, 2018) could be regarded truly as a symbol of the national aspiration to be progressive in ICTs, providing economic incentives for local companies to be more innovative. The technological venue aims to attract more young people to the profession and inviting best specialists in the area from all over the world to teach, do research and share their knowledge in Estonia. It could be regarded as an ideal example of technological incubator for various start-ups, including open data-driven ones. For example, such famous ICT projects as Cybernetica, Starship Technologies, Ektaco, and SMIT operate on the territory on the park.

In general, all these conditions create a favorable social environment to develop various technological platforms and open data projects that, as a rule, demands an increased level of participation from, first of all, local civic communities, i.e., independent developers and technically savvy citizens (Bataineh & Abu-Shanab, 2016; Lee, Almirall, & Wareham, 2015; Puussaar, Johnson, Montague, James, & Wright, 2018; Townsend, 2013). It is especially important in the open data-driven environment, which requires a certain readiness of local communities to reuse various government and corporate datasets as a raw material in independently developed digital solutions in order to fully harness the socioeconomic potential of the phenomena.

3.2.3 Political Environment: The Promise of Open Government and Digital Democracy

Political contexts also play an important role in the development of open data agendas in government. Since the moment Estonia reestablished its independence after the collapse of the USSR in 1991, this nation has striven to build a country that would be based on principles of Western-style parliamentary democracy, respect of human rights and development of civil society (Smith, 2013b; Taagepera, 2018) in contrast to the totalitarian traditions of communist governance that it was once forced to establish shortly after the Soviet occupation in 1940. A really strong aspiration of Estonians to build not only economically prosperous nation but also politically transparent and collaborative state based on ideals of open society has provided a truly favorable environment to develop various digital projects that were aimed at promoting democracy in an electronic manner. Whether it is in embracing citizen-centered e-government (Martens, 2010) or building cost-effective Internet-driven voting systems (Krimmer, Duenas-Cid, Krivonosova, Vinkel, & Koitmae, 2018), the intrinsic focus on solutions that promote democracy in a digital manner made this country politically much stronger.

In this regard, the public support of various e-government solutions helps to create a beneficial political atmosphere in public agencies and organizations to value innovations and new approaches in management. In this regard, the promotion of digital agendas in domestic politics has become a strategy of national priority in this Baltic country and any prospective and economically viable ideas and practical developments that could help to make it technologically better are welcome, regardless of whether they come from civil servants, citizens or businesses. These political signals create a really promising ideological platform to boost political participation and collaboration in the area. It is especially important to promote such a mutually beneficial partnership with civil society when it comes to the advancement of open data as a political phenomenon since the main driver of the concept is civic engagement (Dyson, 2013; Johnson & Robinson, 2014; Mergel, Kleibrink, & Sörvik, 2018; Temiz & Brown, 2017). After all, any advance of open government phenomena or, as it is often referred to, Government 2.0 (Boughzala, Janssen, & Assar, 2015; Khan, 2015; Wirtz & Birkmeyer, 2015) should be evaluated through the prism of civic participation where citizen-to-government transactions themselves are conducted in an interactive two-way manner.

In general, a strong and consistent political and, more importantly, economic support of related civic initiatives at the national level by the Estonian government could potentially be a good institutional prerequisite to promote open data-driven platforms, too, especially in peer-to-peer and e-participation domains of digital governance where financial uncertainty, latent bureaucratic resistance of public sector to be genuinely open, public inertia and lack of grass-root trends in advancing e-collaboration and, more importantly, traditional monopoly of government over decision making in the area could be regarded as primary challenges in advancing the phenomenon as a sustainable concept (Crusoe & Melin, 2018; Karkin, 2014; Mergel, 2018; Nielsen & Krimmer, 2015; Wirtz, Piehler, Thomas, & Daiser, 2016).

3.2.4 The International Environment: The Promise of Global Cooperation in the Area

The international context is another important aspect of open data politics in Estonia. The active outreach of technology-driven public sector solutions in a more global sense is widely regarded as part of the indirect nation branding strategy that would potentially offer some practical dividends, for example, in attracting more investments and skilled professionals and improving a technological and, more importantly, economic image of the country in the international arena. In this regard, the advocacy of a wide range of digital projects and start-ups through the international arena, which is supported by the government, businesses and local communities, helps the nation to be constantly on the forefront of global digital politics agendas.

For example, a special e-residency program, which is designed to be used by all eligible foreign citizens (Kotka, Vargas, & Korjus, 2015; Prause, 2016; Tanel & Sandra, 2015) could be regarded as the first attempt to globalize many of Estonian digital services (Kotka & Liiv, 2015). The access to various interactive cross-border e-government and e-commerce platforms through the e-residence status could be interesting for potential foreign investors, technology enthusiasts and start-up angels. One more global initiative, which is highly praised by the international community, is the establishment of Estonian data embassies (Robinson & Martin, 2017). The key goal of this special project is to ensure better information security of various digital transactions, which are mundanely conducted in the ecosystem of digital state. Resorting to cloud technologies, the data embassies allow Estonian authorities to host, access and update datasets and services from secure information hubs, which are situated outside the territorial borders of the country.

This measure could presumably help to minimize the threat of data siege and tampering into national databases from third countries. Along with the widespread use of blockchain technologies in e-government and e-voting platforms, these cloud solutions help to create a more robust, highly encrypted and technologically much safer information ecosystem upon which a true digital state and information society could be built. In this regard, the general cyber defense policy adopted by Estonian authorities and, in particular, Cyber Command team in army has been culminated in the development of so-called e-military strategy aimed to defend the sovereignty of national information and communication technology facilities and networks from potential foreign cyber attacks.

Estonia was one of the first nations to adopt a comprehensive set of preventive measures to achieve the goal, providing a regulatory and organizational playground for future developments in the digitalization of defense forces. The field of cyber warfare is widely regarded in government and military as a matter of national priority. Therefore, authorities pay special attention to the protection of public data hubs, constantly monitoring related transactions, which are conducted within various centralized and highly integrated databases. In this regard, the adoption of these cyber defense solutions in Estonia could be regarded as a harbinger of strong digital state that other nations could refer to in building similar nationwide information security systems in the future.

One more aspect that directly related to the development of the open data concept in Estonia was the commitments that the national government took when it joined the Open Government Partnership (OGP) in (2012). The commitments explicitly required the promotion of various e-participation initiatives from all member states, among which open data played a crucial role (OGP, 2012). In this regard, the political obligations to advocate more transparent and collaborative government through the initiative have provided a really promising ideological platform to globalize open government strategies all over the world. This universal platform helps to disseminate the best aspects of open data politics in a truly cross-border manner, offering strong incentives for all member states to advance further in this direction by learning, sharing and networking with each other.

This is probably one of the reasons why so many nations seek to cooperate with Estonia, especially in the area of public sector innovations and are particularly interested in studying various Estonian e-government projects. As a result, the technology-driven agenda is beginning to play an ever-increasing role even in the foreign policy of the country. The Japanese-Estonian Dialogues on ICT Policy and Cyber Security that are held regularly both in Tokyo and Tallinn, the digital government cooperation with the United Arab Emirates, Azerbaijan, Ukraine, Moldova, Kyrgyzstan, Kazakhstan and with many other countries (Cornwell, 2015; The Office of the Kazakh Prime Minister, 2018; Vahtra-Hellat, 2015) not to mention that Estonia also headquarters the NATO cyber defense center and the European Agency for the Operational Management of large-scale IT Systems in the Area of Freedom, Security and Justice (EULISA, 2018), all these initiatives are just few great examples of what the promising international cooperation in the area could offer. Such cooperation was especially intensified during the Estonian EU presidency in the second half of 2017 when digital government agendas were actively advocated by this Nordic country throughout continental Europe.

Furthermore, one of the interesting aspects of the developments in this direction is a really close relationship with Finland, with which Estonia shares common linguistic and historical roots. In this regard, a really close cultural and geographical proximity of two fraternal nations has predetermined an intensive cooperation in many ICT-related areas, including in telecommunications and open source software industry, where Finland has strong positions not only in Europe but also in the world. One of the aspirations is to develop a cross-border digital and highly interactive network of the real-time economy (RTE) ecosystem that would help both Estonian and Finnish businesses to easily operate in either country without any bureaucratic obstacles (OECD, 2015), including in a cross-urban manner (Soe & Drechsler, 2018). The geographical nearness of Helsinki and Tallinn provides a highly cost-effective playground to experiment in the area and integrate many of e-commerce and even e-government platforms in an interactive way with an ambitious goal to create a single business information ecosystem between two cities.

Generally, as it was demonstrated in the review of the Estonian country context, all these preconditions to advance technology-driven policy agendas create truly favorable economic, political, social and even international environments for the exchange of knowledge in promoting related digital government solutions, including open data-driven ones. They are all reflected, respectively, in the presence of developed information society and wide range of digital solutions in public administration, advocacy of key values of civil society and respect of human rights in the political arena, aspirations to build a Nordic model of social democracy in

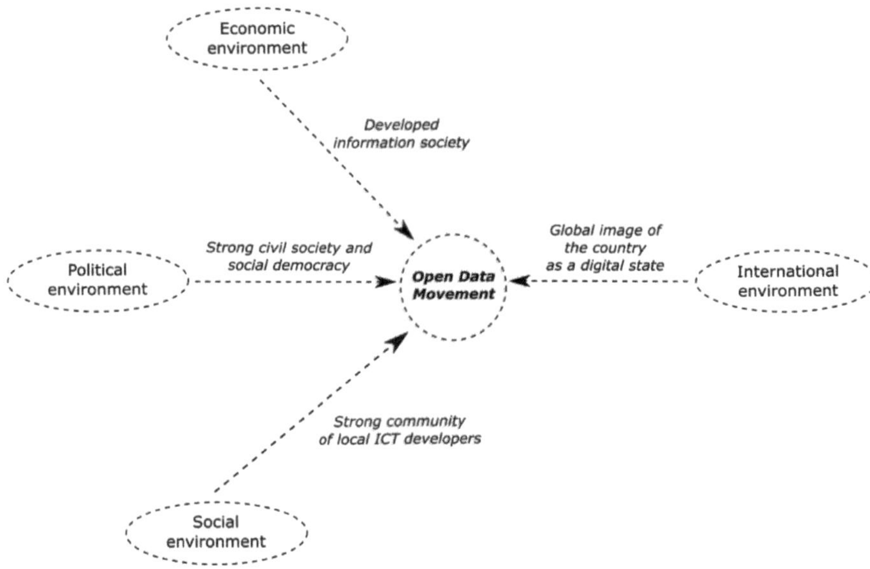

Fig. 3.2 The key environments of the open data movement in Estonia. *Source* Own illustration

economy, a striving community of local developers in a technological sense and, finally, a global image of the country as a poster boy of digital state that helps to globalize and commercialize many of the electronic solutions in international settings (see Fig. 3.2).

3.3 Open Data Regulation: The Focus on Freedom of Information Laws

The analysis of freedom of information and e-government laws is a main source of data that helps to understand the adoption of related open data policies from a strategic point of view. In this regard, the Estonian Public Information Act, which was adopted in 2000 as a local version of the universal freedom of information act (FOIA), is widely regarded by almost all stakeholders as a key strategic regulatory document to authorize publication of government datasets at all institutional levels. The amendments made to the law in 2007, 2011 and, especially, 2012 were explicitly aimed to promote the principles of open state and regulate the reuse of open government data. For example, the article # 4 of the act says that "[the] access to information shall be ensured for every person in the quickest and easiest manner possible" and "without charge unless payment for the direct expenses relating to the release of the information is prescribed by law." It is necessary to note that the sub-section #3 of article 4 clearly endorses the use of public open government platforms by both national and local public agencies. There is only one exception from the rule. The publication of the datasets in any form should not disclose information about private life of Estonians and must ensure protection of copyright (The Public Information Act, 2000).

Furthermore, in addition to the reactive mechanism of FOIA, which usually provides private access to government information only after citizens and legal entities send an official request form, the law denotes in detail, especially in articles # 28 and # 29, what type of data public agencies could now *proactively* disclose. This could be done through either publishing in local media outlets or storing in special digital data platforms. Taking into account the fact that Estonia is a typical unitary state with a really centralized ecosystem of e-government and regulation, the document has an equal force on the territory of the whole country. This fact greatly simplifies the adoption of open data-driven implementation strategies by all public and private stakeholders both at national and local levels.

In addition to the Public Information Act, several regulatory laws such as the Principles of the Estonian Information Policy, which was approved as early as 1998 and its later version—the Principles of the Estonian Information Policy for 2004–2006 as well as the Information Society Services Act adopted in 2004 and the Estonian Information Society Strategy 2013 also partly regulate the work with government information in public domain (Björklund, 2016; Czosseck, Ottis & Talihärm, 2013; Kalvet, 2007; Krull, 2003; Loit & Harro-Loit, 2012). These documents provide an additional legal and political basis to promote open data-driven public sector reforms in various sectors of economy.

3.4 The Analysis of Networking Activities Among Key Stakeholders of the Open Data Movement

3.4.1 Public Sector as a Datasets Provider and Promoter of Open Data Policies

First of all, it is necessary to mention that specifics and traditions of public administration and governance in Estonia have predetermined a leading role of central government in almost all technology-driven public sector reforms there, especially in creating various e-government, e-voting, and e-participation systems. Public sector is also a number one provider of open data at both national and local levels of government and a key promoter of related outreaching activities. All members of national government play their own role in advancing the concept at their instances both domestically and internationally, whether it is in the office of the prime minister, parliament (*Riigikogu* in Estonian), ministries or local municipalities. Such government agencies as the Estonian Information System Authority which develops and administers many e-government platforms, including X-Road, e-voting, intra-governmental document and government data exchange ecosystems such as DHX and X-tee (EISA, 2018), and the Estonian Ministry of Economic Affairs and Communications (MEAC, 2018), which provides political supervision in the area, are among the most important stakeholders of the open data movement at the national level. Although the municipalities of such cities as Tallinn and Tartu also participate in providing additional datasets to local communities, the role of the central government in advancing the concept at various institutional levels is overwhelming, given the unitary nature of the Estonian public administration system.

In this regard, public procurement of innovations plays quite an important role in the area (Kalvet & Lember, 2010), providing certain administrative incentives for government bodies to be more collaborative in developing related digital public projects. As a result, almost all agencies participate in various open government initiatives in reforming public sector by, first of all, preparing, cataloging and publishing their datasets in machine-readable formats. They often cooperate with other stakeholders from non-governmental and business sectors in order to better harness an economic and political potential of the concept, whether it is in helping third-party ICT-specialists to develop applications, researching the topic in academia, consulting or co-funding various development projects in the area. The close partnership with a wide range of technological companies, non-governmental players and international organizations and even with local mass media in outreaching the projects in the public sphere helps to advance the concept as a truly multidimensional phenomenon.

3.4.2 The Non-governmental Sector as an Advocate of Digital Democracy

The participation of the non-governmental sector is one of the most important elements in advancing open data phenomena. The reuse of government datasets demands active participation from the part of local non-commercial stakeholders that could support independent developers and technically savvy citizens in promoting their open data-driven projects and start-ups. In this respect, it is necessary to note that Estonia has built one of the most transparent societies in the world that enjoys a soaring level of the Internet neutrality, freedom of press and associations, which creates a favorable environment to develop various digital civic engagement and participatory initiatives in the non-governmental sector. The developed civil society is very active and flexible in partnership with both businesses and government agencies in promoting a wide range of civic initiatives and platforms in the area. These projects are all aimed to make governance in Estonia better and more democratic, including by resorting to the power of open data-driven public sector innovations.

Local non-governmental organizations are especially active in academic and research areas, for example, in studying the best international practices in the area or generating new ideas on how to further the open data-driven government and public administration. Such non-governmental organizations as the e-Governance Academy or the Praxis Think Tank (Praxis, 2018) provide really valuable knowledge and expertise in the area to national government and business sector, other NGOs and think tanks, independent developers and technological companies, international organizations and even foreign governments, consulting and helping them to develop and improve the operation of various digital projects and accelerate related public sector innovations. For example, e-Governance Academy, which is based in Tallinn, provides on a regular basis trainings and seminars for e-government policymakers and practitioners in various parts of the world such as those on e-democracy, cloud solutions in e-government, smart city technologies, cyber-security measures in public administration, etc. (EGA, 2018).

3.4.3 Local Academia as an Incubator of New Ideas in Government Technology

The participation of local academic communities in advancing digital politics agendas in Estonia and beyond is hard to overestimate since they are directly engaged in the development of many of the related strategies and their expert opinion is taken into account by policymakers. The academic communities in three leading institutions of tertiary education in Estonia, namely, the Tallinn University of Technology, which is also known among locals as TalTech, University of Tartu and the Estonian Information Technology College play a decisive role in conceptually developing and promoting many e-government, e-participation, e-voting, e-military, e-school, e-medicine, e-trade, e-infrastructure and recently also open government models. They participate not only in researching various political and socioeconomic aspects of the phenomenon that is gaining increasing popularity today in this country but also in providing consultative assistance and expertise to both public and private sectors on the topic. This makes Estonian academia an active stakeholder of almost all ICT-driven public sector reforms.

In this respect, the Tallinn University of Technology, along with the University of Koblenz at Landau (Germany) and Victoria University of Wellington (New Zealand) is one of the rarest academic institutions in the world that provides special education in government technology curricula, offering even postgraduate master and doctoral degrees in the field (TUT, 2018), which is specifically aimed at preparing professionals in e-government, e-voting, e-participation and other related majors. Almost all foreign graduates of these education programs are directly engaged in advancing digital government agendas in their home countries, either as policymakers, practitioners or researchers, creating a truly global alumni network that advocates, updates and disseminates knowledge about the latest developments in the area. In this connection, a number of research projects that study the topic of digital technologies in public sector reforms make the university one of the leading research centers in the area in Europe and beyond.

3.4.4 The Journalistic Community as an Ideological Promoter of Open Government Philosophy

The media sector plays a crucial role in the development of domestic Estonian politics, acting as an independent watchman of all public reforms in various sectors of economy. A free and partisan-free editorial policy adopted by many local media outlets creates a wholesome environment for the emergence of investigative journalism that critically monitors and reviews all decisions made by public agencies, including in e-government areas. In this regard, a really patriotic journalistic community is another important stakeholder of the open data movement in Estonia, too, which is very active in covering and publicly debating on the topic both in print and electronic media outlets. The role of local mass media is really crucial not only in outreaching various open data projects and other e-government initiatives but also in popularizing related computer and technology training. The key target audience is the Estonian young generation. By informing citizens and residents about new digital projects and platforms that are implemented today by both public and non-governmental sectors, the journalistic community plays a crucial educational and promotional role in the area, acting as an advocate or relentless critic of current policies in the area.

It is necessary to say that for many years Estonia has been universally regarded as a model of open society and freedom of speech. Several times this nation has been recognized among the top ten in the World Press Freedom Index (Reporters Without Borders, 2018) and the Global Freedom on the Net Index (The Freedom House, 2018). Digital politics and data-driven journalism are among popular topics of discussion in local media outlets. The access to state-held information is guaranteed in local media laws and is advocated by all representatives of the profession as a beacon of investigative reporting and independent journalism. In this regard, local journalists understand the importance of public relations in promoting knowledge about various e-government-driven projects and civic open data-driven start-ups to further the successful development of the nation. It is interesting to note that almost all media portals provide their content additionally in English, sharing the news on the topic with the whole world. Such public and private independent media projects as the e-Estonia media platform (e-Estonia, 2016), the Estonian World (EW, 2016), the Estonian Public Broadcasting Corporation (ERR, 2016), and many other multimedia initiatives systematically cover various topics related to digital politics, critically assessing all initiatives proposed by public sector in the area and often resorting to the analysis of data provided by whistleblowers from both public and private sectors of economy. Such new revelations and data are actively discussed then in social media networks with the participation of local civic communities. There is no restriction on the use of social media platforms in Estonian laws and the phenomenon of digital activism aimed to criticize e-government policymakers is highly respected by all stakeholders as an additional source of reference and advice for public sector to improve.

In this regard, journalistic and academic communities often work together in investigating the critical aspects in the development of the Estonian digital government ecosystem, especially if the topics are related to the defects in various information security and data management platforms. For example, in early 2017 local journalistic communities with the help of researcher from University of Tartu Arnis Paršovs played a decisive role in outreaching critical information about flaws in Estonia's e-government infrastructure, which suffered from a presumably intentional chip malfunction in government-issued ID cards (Kund & Pau, 2018). This technical mistake could have led to potentially serious security breaches. Therefore, government agencies had to recall security signatures from more than 760,000 ID cards until new security certificates were renewed. It was one of the major blows in the whole ecosystem of e-government for more than two decades of its operation in this country.

3.4.5 ICT-Developers as a Focal Point of Open Data-Driven Networking Activities

It is impossible to build a sustainable digital society without an army of professionals in information technology, who would run and maintain all related digital platforms. The amendments made to the Estonian Electronic Communications Act in 2014 that were aimed to further liberalization and a fair competition in telecommunications resulted in the widespread popularization of Internet neutrality policy among local mobile operators and numerous Internet service providers. In this respect, Estonia could be proud to have a really developed, socially active and highly competitive labor market of computer specialists and engineers. Furthermore, philanthropic and patriotic feelings are highly esteemed and nurtured by local community of independent developers, who often prefer to call themselves as technically savvy citizens. They are ready to share their expertise and knowledge and help both government and civil society to make the public sector and local economy of the country better and more cost-effective, including by resorting to the promise of open data.

In this respect, the earlier mentioned Tallinn Tehnopol Park is a really popular place among many local developers, designers, coders, and software testers for professional networking and concerted development of various technological projects and data-driven start-ups, sharing and exchanging of knowledge, collaboration, and competition in related areas such as the promotion of linked data, big data, and mashup technologies. Another networking platform is provided by the so-called Garage48 hackathon project, a meeting of local developers which is convened regularly and represented by a number of professionals and engineers from various parts of the country and beyond. The Garage48 Foundation that runs the project was established in 2010 and has become an extremely popular venue for Estonian developers to launch their start-ups and projects in the area This networking platform is now gaining also a regional importance in other Baltic states, neighboring Belarus and Ukraine and even in Central Asia and Africa (The Garage48 Project, 2018), transforming this initiative into a truly international networking platform for young computer programmers in these regions.

In this regard, a local community of independent developers plays a crucial role in promoting various regional digital collaborative projects as a multidimensional ICT phenomenon, including in actively propagating philosophy of data philanthropy among its peers. In general, the open data movement provides an effective collaborative and networking platform to boost cooperation and mutually beneficial activities in the area among various stakeholders such as government agencies (e.g., in consistently releasing datasets in special public depositories), academic communities and local non-governmental organizations (e.g., in providing related research, consultations and exchange of knowledge and expertise), journalistic communities (e.g., in raising public awareness about the phenomena in both public and private sectors of economy), and, more importantly, developers (e.g., in reusing open data to create various projects and start-ups in the area) (see Fig. 3.3).

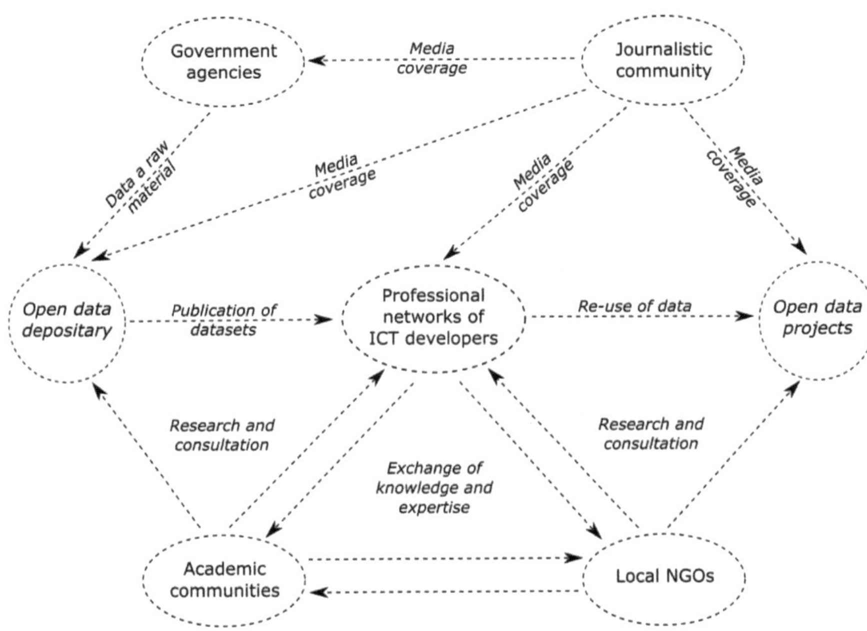

Fig. 3.3 Open data as a multidimensional collaborative and networking movement in Estonia. *Source* Own illustration

3.5 The Policy Review of the Open Data Movement in Estonia: Understanding Implementation Policies

The policy review of the open data movement is based on the analysis of implementation strategies adopted by Estonian e-government policymakers in outreaching key public values of the concept at various institutional levels. In this regard, the progress of the phenomena is first of all reviewed and evaluated in accordance with three most important political benchmarks of open government philosophy, namely transparency, participation and collaboration (Lathrop & Ruma, 2010). Such investigation is done through the analysis of, respectively, open data policies aimed at advocating key values of government transparency and outreaching reuse of open data in civic and private sectors of economy; the study of related participatory trends among citizens and, more importantly, close examination of collaborative open data-driven projects, which are usually independently developed by local civic or business communities.

3.5.1 Institutional Focus on Digital Centralization

In the context of such unitary state as Estonia, the leading role of central authorities is crucial in promoting almost all digital government platforms. In this regard, the implementation of all technology-driven projects in public sector is accompanied with a highly centralized approach in the administration of related projects. This is especially evident in the management of highly interconnected national databases, the operation of public digital platforms and implementation of executive policies in the area. For example, e-government, e-voting, e-participation, e-collaboration, e-taxation, and many other initiatives are operated within the framework of the single national digital identification ecosystem, also known as *X-road* (Anthes, 2015; Kalja, 2002; Kalvet, 2012).

The national open data platform is also promoted in a really centralized manner (ODP, 2015). There is no separate open data project that publishes government information at different institutional levels. In this regard, Estonian authorities have resorted to a truly innovative administrative practice in building-related digital platforms. Such centralized approach is rarely seen today in the world, taking into account the fact that many open data projects are usually implemented at three different bureaucratic levels, namely national, provincial and local ones, which, in addition, often are distributed among separate ministerial and institutional organizations, making the promotion of the concept extremely complex and cumbersome, especially at federal levels, e.g., in the USA, Canada, Australia, many European and Latin American nations.

Therefore, the promotion of multiple and open data projects at different national, regional, local, institutional, public and private levels create an extremely diverse multidimensional realm of the open government movement in these federal nations,

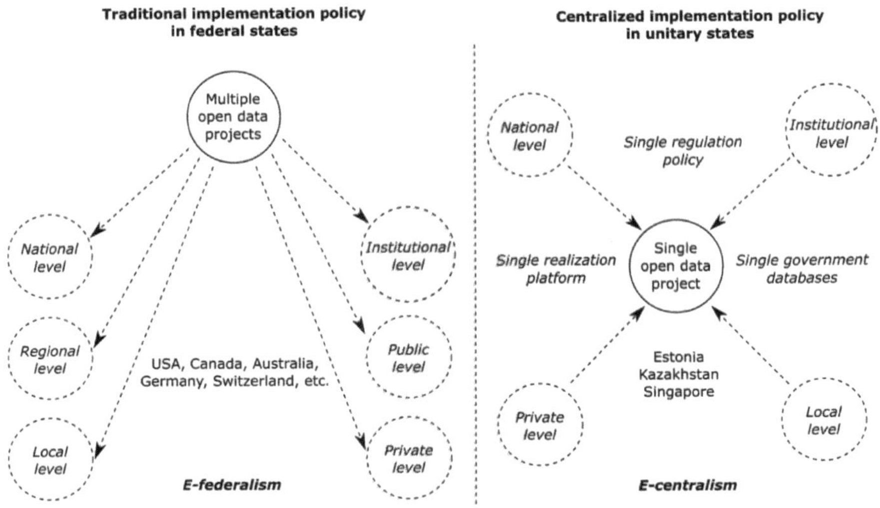

Fig. 3.4 Institutional differences between traditional decentralized and centralized open data implementation policies. *Source* Own illustration

indicating to the existence of the phenomena, which could be tentatively called *e-federalism* (Kassen, 2015). In this respect, Estonia as other unitary states such as Singapore or Kazakhstan has adopted a cardinally different approach of *e-centralism* which is characterized by its simplicity and cost-effectiveness since the promotion of the open data concept at all levels is carried out in a strictly centralized manner in regulating, implementing and managing databases at all institutional levels of government (see Fig. 3.4).

3.5.2 Open Data-Driven Learning Philosophy

Another interesting feature of the open data movement in Estonia is adoption of special education and outreaching policies, which are all aimed at providing instructions and guides on how to process, reuse or reformat government datasets in accordance with local socioeconomic needs. For example, these training materials explain how developers and technically savvy citizens could easily create third-party open data-driven initiatives and mobile applications in an organizational and technological manner, explaining in detail all the actual stages of development procedure. These guides also indirectly popularize philosophy of sharing and collective learning, encouraging the use of open source software and free computer formats of datasets in various forums and hackathon events. For example, the platform of the open data community that monitors the advancement of the official open data project in Estonia (ODC, 2018) publishes hyperlinks to special file depositories where developers could find and freely download software tools, which could be then helpful in developing various open data-driven start-ups and initiatives (The community tools project, 2015).

The project itself is supported by a number of public and non-governmental organizations such as the state-sponsored National Foundation of Civil Society (NFCS, 2015), the Enterprise Estonia (EE, 2015), and the private Open Estonia Foundation (OEF, 2015) among others. Moreover, the official open data platform provides personalization, interactive alerts and many other features (ODP, 2015) that greatly simplify the technological interface of the whole ecosystem, potentially allowing even to automate the development of related third-party open data-driven projects and independent collaborative and civic engagement platforms (e.g., through the automatic update of datasets in a real-time manner), making the initiative extremely useful for system engineers, programmers, interface designers, coders and code testers.

3.6 The Content Analysis of Independent Open Data-Driven Projects

The investigation of independent open data-driven initiatives is probably the most important aspect not only of the content analysis but also of the whole case study research. After all, the implementation of the concept, i.e., the reuse of government data is unthinkable without the participation of third parties, namely, independent developers, local businesses and sometimes technically savvy citizens. These three stakeholders not only process and improve in a collaborative manner the quality of available datasets retrieved from official digital depositories and e-government platforms as a raw material but also create their own independent information and interactive applications. This, in turn, could complement the existing systems of official e-government services or even offer a completely new range of transactional products, closing all available gaps in the information market. It is this surplus product and reinvigorating environment of close collaboration between government and private stakeholders that could generate the main public value of the open data concept, which is the growth of civic engagement and public sector innovations.

3.6.1 The Riigiraha Project: Ensuring Public Scrutiny of Government Fiscal Activities at Local Levels

Probably, one of the most popular open data-driven projects is a Riigiraha initiative, which was launched in 2014 with the help of the Estonian Ministry of Finance in order to engage citizens in tracking all information related to financial operations at the level of local governments and municipalities in every region of the country (The Riigiraha project, 2015). One of the most promising features of the initiative, which provides access to various open data-based analytical and visualization tools, is an opportunity to monitor all government related revenues and spending both at national and local levels for a particular time period. The project allows tracking such details as taxpayer's basis, operating outcomes, investment activities, monthly salaries of elected and appointed civil servants, spending on social programs, and other financial statistics, using comprehensive yet clear and easily comparable graphics, charts, and interactive maps embedded in the platform.

Another useful feature of the project is that it also provides a guide for citizens (Jõgi, 2014) on how to use more advanced instruments of analysis both in Estonian and English languages such as filtering of data in accordance with the time period, the name of the local municipality or county, type of revenues and spending, etc. It also allows comparing the datasets and even building personalized charts, which presumably could be extremely helpful technically for researchers, students and journalists in studying, understanding or investigating the situation with public finances at local levels, monitoring potential discrepancies in public revenues and expenses, tracking suspicious fiscal operations or mismanagement of public spending. It is interesting to note that the project could be regarded as somewhat a reincarnation of previously quite a popular initiative entitled—a *Riigipilv project*—that was designed and launched in 2012. Created in partnership with the private telecommunications provider Elion (ERR, 2012), it was aimed to promote transparency of government through public scrutiny of budget spending by local authorities in various sectors of economy (ePSI, 2014).

3.6.2 The Valitsemise Valvurid Project: Monitoring the Fulfillment of Electoral Promises

Another civic engagement initiative that is based on the use of the open data principle but more in the political domain is a Valitsemise Valvurid project. The direct translation of the words from Estonian is "the government watchdog." In this respect, the key idea of this collaborative platform is to help citizens to easily track how elected officials and political groups fulfill their election promises and campaign programs and monitor the overall performance of national government in various areas (The Valitsemise Valvurid Project, 2015). The start-up is supported by the Open Estonia Foundation and relies heavily on technical and expert assistance from the local network of independent developers, academia and non-governmental organizations. Currently, the project, which is based on evaluations and ratings provided by a number of independent observers, tracks the promises given by elected government during the last parliamentary elections.

It also offers a number of useful filtering and visualization tools that help to check the progress of the current government in accomplishing the promises in various areas such as social protection, infrastructure, employment, family policy, agriculture, and transportation. This information provides mass media and members of local neighborhoods with a really effective instrument of public control and scrutiny that helps Estonia to advance further in building a truly transparent and collaborative public sector, using sophisticated yet highly cost-effective innovative open data-driven projects and platforms.

At the moment, the Valitsemise Valvurid tracks more than 500 government activities in an extremely wide range of areas, monitoring them in accordance with such important benchmarks as the relationship of current public sector reforms to the previously given formal promises, locating any delays or failures in fulfilling the government programs, and assessing the reviews of independent observers in the area. Among the most active observers are such non-governmental and nonprofit organizations as Praxis think tank, the Network of Estonian Nonprofit Organizations (NENO, 2016), the Estonian Village Movement (EVM, 2016), the Tallinn-based International Centre for Defense and Security (ICDS, 2015), the Stockholm Environment Institute (SEI, 2015), the Tartu-based Institute of Baltic Studies (IBS, 2015), and many other non-governmental organizations as well as legal entities and individual experts. The platform also welcomes feedback from local civic communities on its official social media accounts in Facebook and Twitter, where citizens can share and comment on current evaluations and performance ratings, contributing to a greater public awareness about the government activity in various sectors of economy and making the public sector more responsive to the needs of people.

3.6.3 The Meieraha Project: Tracking Public Spending and Disbursement of Budget Assignations

One more popular open data-driven project is the Meieraha initiative, which is aimed at helping the civil society to track and scrutinize local public income and spending. The project's name—*meie raha,* which literally means "our money" in Estonian, is quite a right denomination for the independent platform. Whether it is in tracking government spending in the education area, comparing the amount of budget assignations on healthcare and environmental protection or understanding the role of social welfare programs in decreasing poverty, the open data-driven platform provides different types of visualizations on budget expenditures in various areas of economy (The Meieraha Project, 2015). The project makes the scrutiny of any spending in the public sector in Estonia easily traceable and transparent and could be regarded as an additional tool of reference and statistical analysis for local residents, journalists, researchers, and non-governmental organizations. In this regard, one of the most interesting features of the platform is an opportunity to use a tax distribution calculator that helps to understand where the money that taxpayers are paying every month exactly goes. Another useful feature of the project is a city budget visualization tool that could be helpful in analyzing the structure of local public spending. In addition, the official account of the project in Facebook helps visitors to receive alerts, share and comment about the visualization tools and receive the latest news on the topic.

It is necessary to note that the project itself, which claims to be independently developed and not financed by any political player in Estonia, was launched by volunteers from local developers during the above mentioned Garage48 hackathons in early 2011 and currently supported by the Open Estonia Foundation, a famous NGO that helps local civic engagement projects to promote open government, citizens collaboration and e-participation (OEF, 2015). It is interesting that the creators of the Meieraha project, which provides almost all information equally in both Estonian and English languages, have ambitions to popularize the idea also as a budget tracking platform in many Central and Eastern European countries. Such outreach activities could be achieved through a really extensive network of the Open Society Foundation in the region (Oll, 2015). Harnessing the international dimension of the open data-driven cooperation among regional non-governmental players, local developers and technically savvy citizens, the project could facilitate the development of universal cost-effective platforms in the area.

In general, these kinds of open data-driven projects make Estonia one of the most advanced nations in the world in ensuring the principle of transparency in e-government-related areas, which rely heavily not only on direct support from public sector but also collaboration and participation from non-government players and, more importantly, communities of independent developers and technically savvy citizens. The latter are true pioneers of the trend. They harness a promising potential of open data-driven civic engagement, whether it is in acquiring additional knowledge and data from local academic communities, expertise from computer specialists and businesses, receiving feedback from peers in local civic communities or securing funding from various global, national or regional non-governmental organizations and development funds.

As a result, the implementation of these projects is a real example of cooperative and mutually beneficial nature of the open data concept. All these factors contribute greatly to the promotion of conceptually self-sustainable mechanisms in many open data-driven projects which are promoted today in Estonia. The public sector acts not only as a dataset provider but also as an ultimate destination for all feedback options that are coming from such projects. Moreover, the concept allows the non-governmental sector to track the activity of government in the area and, if necessary, provide assistance, expertise, and consultations to the latter on related topics. In this regard, citizens not only act as mere consumers of the open data-driven services but also as providers of additional information and new datasets to further the concept as a collaborative project.

3.7 Key Challenges of the Open Data Movement

3.7.1 Lack of Economic Incentives and Fundraising Basis

Estonia has made a great job in transforming the national economy since the moment it regained its independence in 1991, especially in reforming its financial system, diversifying income sources and building new infrastructural basis to promote various industries, whether it is in information technology, agriculture or transportation sectors. However, despite the fact the level of the gross domestic product (GDP) per capita is higher than in other Baltic states and it is steadily rising, it is still significantly lower than in many other European nations. The modest opportunities to find funding in the ICT area at local levels make many successful and established projects to move abroad in search of new markets and capital despite the fact that government creates a really favorable political environment and economic conditions to promote various technological start-ups. In this regard, open data-driven projects, which promotion presumably requires the presence of robust funding opportunities, first of all, from the part of citizens, make it feasible to further only if there is a systematic support from local non-governmental organizations and partly public sector rather than from local communities, which currently are not ready to fund such projects.

Policy recommendation

One of the possible solutions could be found in the creation of special pan-European development funds that would support various civic open data-driven initiatives not only in Estonia but also in other transitional societies, for example, in Latvia and Lithuania. In fact, there is no need for regional authorities to invent a special mechanism of such assistance. They could apply all available financial schemes that are widely used today at the union level in order to raise money for such funds, boosting the open data movement in all emerging economies in the region. Taking into account the fact that all these Baltic nations are full member states of the European Union, the centralized funding in providing such assistance or grant support from Brussels could play a decisive role in finding more sustainable mechanisms to support local civic open data-driven projects. Such assistance could be provided not only to a wide community of independent developers and open data enthusiasts but also to other stakeholders, e.g., non-governmental organizations, think tanks, mass media and business start-ups in e-government and e-commerce areas. These stakeholders are intrinsically interested in the successful implementation of the concept as a promising platform that would allow them to network, share experience and obtain new knowledge in a cross-border manner. For example, various grant schemes, organization of master classes and hackathons for independent developers at the continental level would create a new favorable ecosystem to advance various open data-driven initiatives and projects, eventually leading to the increase in public sector innovations in many transitional economies in Europe.

3.7.2 No Participation of Local Business Communities

Another aspect of the controversial economic environment is a relatively low level of corporate spending on research and development in comparison with other countries in the EU (Eurostat, 2014; The Statistical Agency of Estonia, 2014) and, more importantly, almost zero participation of business communities in supporting local open data-driven projects, which potentially could boost further technological and scientific progress in the area both in private sector and academia. This could also be generally conducive to the advancement of open data-driven projects since such initiatives are often indirectly funded through grants and direct investments in the non-governmental sector and academic research centers. In addition, the possible increased cooperation between Estonian corporations, research institutes, think tanks and developers could help local entrepreneurs to apply and run their projects at a new higher level of quality, both in terms of cost-effectiveness and orientation at achieving better results. Furthermore, the promotion of open data-driven projects in sciences could provide a new impetus to develop local economy in many ways, whether it is in finding the best strategies on how to harness the economic potential of the concept, which, according to even the modest estimations, could be really promising and rewarding in business environment, or developing open data-driven platforms that would provide new opportunities to advance more innovative e-government platforms, especially in e-participation.

Policy recommendation

The engagement and publicity really matter in digital society. Therefore, it is important to promote more favorable economic conditions for local businesses to join the open data movement and harness its potential. The ultimate goal is to boost innovations and increase profit as well as popularize better socioeconomic benefits of the concept promotion through extensive media campaigns. By nurturing open data entrepreneurship and attracting global investment angels in the area who could help to implement fully the untapped commercial potential of the concept, it is possible to unlock new market niches in local economy. These new economic opportunities, in turn, could help to create new jobs and potentially open new cost-effective ways to further e-government reforms in this country. One of the possible solutions could be found in creating special tax-free zones for open data-driven start-ups and related business projects in the area. This would provide an attractive venue for domestic and global players in the area to network, cooperate and even create a special international hub for open data innovators in this Baltic nation. Taking into account its previous achievements in technology-driven public sector reforms that later proved to be very pragmatic and cost-effective; Estonia has all socioeconomic preconditions and aptitude to achieve significant results in the area.

3.7.3 *Paradoxical Competition of Open Data Philosophy with E-Government and E-Commerce Ecosystems*

The developed market of various e-government and e-commerce platforms could potentially decrease the socioeconomic environment to promote the open data movement in Estonia. In fact, a high level of user satisfaction in e-government services (OGP, 2015) and provision of an extremely wide range of digital initiatives both in public and private sectors of economy ironically make the promotion of many independent open data-driven products unnecessary and often functionally duplicative to public ones. For the last two decades, these public e-government platforms have filled almost all potentially promising economic niches in many areas and excelled dramatically over time in terms of quality and diversification. Moreover, a key public value of the open data concept—the promotion of philosophy of transparency, participation and collaboration has long ago been embraced in the Estonian public sphere, since almost all government information had been published there even before the introduction of the open data concept in 2009 and by that time this Baltic nation had for decades been regarded as a model of government transparency, freedom of information and digital democracy. In this regard, Estonia has become, to some extent, a victim of its own excellence, incredible scrupulousness and extreme technological sophistication in building a truly ubiquitous digital state.

Policy recommendation

The promotion of open data is all about collaboration. In this respect, looking at the Estonian model of technology-driven reforms, one can see that public and private sectors provide today a wide range of interactive platforms in e-government and e-commerce realms. The digitalization as a technological and also socioeconomic phenomenon has affected almost all spheres of human activity in this country, which, eventually, created a highly centralized well-functioning ecosystem to advance electronic services. In addition, almost all digital products are provided through a very cost-effective single nationwide authorization mechanism, using electronic signatures and other unique identification credentials of citizens and businesses. Policymakers, in this respect, have resorted to the phenomena of digital centralization, which could be rarely seen today in the world. Therefore, as a practical recommendation, in the context of such a highly developed digital state, the provision of any electronic services outside of this e-government ecosystem should be regarded as complementary only. Otherwise, this would force many open data-driven projects promoted today by the non-governmental sector to directly compete with public and private sectors in finding better and often very narrow and specific niches in an extremely developed market of digital services. Such civic projects should, instead, focus on advancing more political aspects of open data such as transparency of government and public scrutiny of its activity rather than just on providing socioeconomic services. These new slots would, in turn, complement the traditional top-down ecosystem of implementation in e-government with new more collaborative, transparent and participatory mechanisms to promote the concept of open data further as, first of all, a tool of digital democracy.

3.8 Summary: Key Findings

This chapter claims to be a policy review that is aimed to understand the development of the open data movement in an unusual context of such ubiquitous digital state as Estonia. The case of this country is especially interesting, taking into account its global image as a pioneer of e-democracy and e-governance. Today, this nation is also inventing its own ways to promote open data initiatives in both public and private sectors of economy. In this regard, analyzing key implementation policies, stakeholders, drivers and barriers of the open data movement in this Baltic country, the author came to the conclusion that the implementation of the open data concept demands completely new mechanisms of promotion, more collaborative and participatory than ever before. As it was observed in the Estonian case, its progress is more dependable on close partnership of government agencies with nonprofit organizations and independent developers rather than on traditional instruments of bureaucratic control and direct funding in implementing related public sector reforms.

This is especially true when it comes to finding competitive niches to promote new open data-driven products and related participatory services. In this regard, it is this atmosphere of civic engagement and collaboration in the non-governmental area that resulted in the emergence of a number of independent projects, which eventually created really favorable conditions to boost related networking activities among such important stakeholders as government agents, journalists, academia, think tanks and technically savvy citizens. Finally, the case of Estonia has also clearly demonstrated the importance of cooperation with the local non-governmental sector and, more importantly, independent developers, which active participation is crucial for the overall progress of the open data movement, to a greater degree, as a networking platform to ensure transparency of government rather than a business incubator.

References

Abu-Shanab, E. A., & Bataineh, L. Q. (2014). Challenges facing e-government projects: how to avoid failure? *International Journal of Emerging Sciences, 4*(4), 207–218.

Ahmad, S. Z., & Khalid, K. (2017). The adoption of M-government services from the user's perspectives: Empirical evidence from the United Arab Emirates. *International Journal of Information Management, 37*(5), 367–379.

Anthes, G. (2015). Estonia: A model for e-government. *Communications of the ACM, 58*(6), 18–20.

Åström, J., Jonsson, M., Hinsberg, H., & Karlsson, M. (2013). *Case studies on e-participation policy*. Sweden, Estonia and Iceland: Praxis Policy Center.
Bakunzibake, P., Grönlund, Å., & Klein, G. O. (2016, September). E-Government implementation in developing countries: Enterprise content management in Rwanda. In *15th IFIP Electronic Government (EGOV)/8th Electronic Participation (ePart) Conference*, Univ Minho, Guimaraes, Portugal, September 5–8, 2016 (pp. 251–259). IOS Press.
Basu, S. (2004). E-government and developing countries: An overview. *International Review of Law Computers & Technology, 18*(1), 109–132.
Bataineh, L., & Abu-Shanab, E. (2016). How perceptions of E-participation levels influence the intention to use E-government websites. *Transforming Government: People Process and Policy, 10*(2), 315–334.
Baum, S., & Mahizhnan, A. (2015). Government-with-you: e-government in Singapore. In *Public affairs and administration: Concepts, methodologies, tools, and applications* (pp. 711–725). IGI Global.
Björklund, F. (2016). E-government and moral citizenship: The case of Estonia. *Citizenship Studies, 20*(6–7), 914–931.
Boughzala, I., Janssen, M., & Assar, S. (2015). *E-government 2.0: Back to reality, a 2.0 application to vet. In Case studies in e-Government 2.0* (pp. 1–14). Springer, Cham.
Chen, A., & Huang, W. (2015). China's E-Government. In *Managing organizational complexities with digital enablement in China: A casebook* (pp. 97–106).
Chen, A. J., Pan, S. L., Zhang, J., Huang, W. W., & Zhu, S. (2009). Managing e-government implementation in China: A process perspective. *Information & Management, 46*(4), 203–212.
Cornwell, A. (2015, October 20). Why Dubai is looking to Estonia to develop a digital city. *The Gulf News*. http://gulfnews.com/business/economy/why-dubai-is-looking-to-estonia-to-develop-a-digital-city-1.1603874. Accessed on: June 10, 2017.
Crusoe, J., & Melin, U. (2018, September). Investigating open government data barriers. In *International Conference on Electronic Government* (pp. 169–183). Springer, Cham.
Czosseck, C., Ottis, R., & Talihärm, A. M. (2013). Estonia after the 2007 cyber attacks: Legal, strategic and organisational changes in cyber security. Case studies in information warfare and security: For researchers, teachers and students, 72.
Dada, D. (2006). The failure of E-government in developing countries: A literature review. *The Electronic Journal of Information Systems in Developing Countries, 26*(1), 1–10.
Drechsler, W. (1995). Estonia in transition. *World Affairs, 157*(3), 111–117.
Drechsler, W., & Madise, Ü. (2004). Electronic voting in Estonia. In *Electronic voting and democracy* (pp. 97–108). Palgrave Macmillan, London.
Dyson, L. (Ed.). (2013). *Beyond transparency: Open data and the future of civic innovation*. Code for America Press.
Ebbers, W. E., Jansen, M. G., & van Deursen, A. J. (2016). Impact of the digital divide on e-government: Expanding from channel choice to channel usage. *Government Information Quarterly, 33*(4), 685–692.
EE. (2015). *The enterprise Estonia Project*. http://www.eas.ee/en. Accessed on: January 25, 2016.
e-Estonia. (2016). *The e-Estonia media Project*. https://e-estonia.com. Accessed on: July 27, 2016.
e-Estonia. (2018). *The Estonian Education Information System*. https://e-estonia.com/solutions/education. Accessed on: November 24, 2018.
EGA. (2018). *The e-Government Academy*. http://www.ega.ee. Accessed on: October 2, 2018.
EISA. (2018). *The Estonian Information System Authority*. https://www.ria.ee/en. Accessed on: November 24, 2018.
ePSI. (2014). *The European Public Sector information platform. Estonia opens up local government financial data via a new dedicated site*. http://www.epsiplatform.eu/content/estonia-opens-local-government-financial-data-new-dedicated-site-0. Accessed on: January 25, 2016.
ERR. (2012). The Estonian Public Broadcasting (ERR). *New system puts local government spending under virtual microscope*. http://news.err.ee/v/scitech/7ee96ac8–05b8-43c9-b60b-38eb0cffc2dd. Accessed on: January 25, 2016.

ERR. (2016). *The Estonian Public Broadcasting Corporation*. http://news.err.ee. Accessed on: December 5, 2016.

EULISA. (2018). The European Agency for the operational management of large-scale IT Systems in the area of freedom, Security and Justice. www.eulisa.europa.eu.

Eurostat. (2014). *Gross domestic expenditure on R&D* http://ec.europa.eu/eurostat/tgm/table.do?tab=table&init=1&plugin=1&language=en&pcode=tsdec320. Accessed on: February 15, 2016.

EVM. (2016). *The Estonian Village Movement* http://kodukant.kovtp.ee. Accessed on: July 12, 2017.

EW. (2016). *The Estonian World Project*. www.estonianworld.com. Accessed on: August 17, 2016.

Gao, X., & Lee, J. (2017). E-government services and social media adoption: Experience of small local governments in Nebraska state. *Government Information Quarterly, 34*(4), 627–634.

Helbig, N., Gil-García, J. R., & Ferro, E. (2009). Understanding the complexity of electronic government: Implications from the digital divide literature. *Government Information Quarterly, 26*(1), 89–97.

Hui, G., & Hayllar, M. R. (2010). Creating public value in e-Government: A public-private-citizen collaboration framework in Web 2.0. *Australian Journal of Public Administration, 69*, 120–131.

IBS. (2015). *The Institute of Baltic Studies*. https://www.ibs.ee/en. Accessed on: December 9, 2015.

ICDS. (2015). *The International Centre for Defense and Security*. http://www.icds.ee. Accessed on: July 12, 2017.

Information Age. (2011). *EU open data strategy promises €40 billion boost*. http://www.information-age.com/technology/information-management/1678798/eu-open-data-strategy-promises-%E2%82%AC40-billion-boost. Accessed on: December 24, 2015.

Internet Live Stats. (2017a). *Estonia Internet Users*. http://www.internetlivestats.com/internet-users/estonia/. Accessed on: December 2, 2018.

Jõgi, A. (2014). *Estonia launches OpenData application for municipalities*. http://www.fin.ee/estonia-launches-opendata-application-for-municipalities. Accessed on: January 25, 2016.

Johnson, P., & Robinson, P. (2014). Civic Hackathons: Innovation, procurement, or civic engagement? *Review of Policy Research, 31*(4), 349–357.

Kalja, A. (2002). The X-road project. A project to modernize Estonia's national databases. *Baltic IT&T Review, 24*, 47–48.

Kalja, A., Põld, J., Robal, T., & Vallner, U. (2011, July). Modernization of the e-government in Estonia. In 2011 *Proceedings of PICMET'11 Technology Management in the Energy Smart World (PICMET)* (pp. 1–7). IEEE.

Kalvet, T. (2004). *The Estonian ICT manufacturing and software industry: Current state and future outlook*. Tallinn: Poliitikauuringute Keskus Praxis.

Kalvet, T. (2007). The Estonian information society developments since the 1990s. PRAXIS.

Kalvet, T. (2012). Innovation: A factor explaining e-government success in Estonia. *Electronic Government, an International Journal, 9*(2), 142–157.

Kalvet, T., & Lember, V. (2010). Risk management in public procurement for innovation: the case of Nordic–Baltic Sea cities. *Innovation–The European Journal of Social Science Research, 23*(3), 241–262.

Kamińska-Korolczuk, K., & Kijewska, B. (2017). Internet in Estonia and Poland. The Routledge companion to global internet histories, 135.

Karkin, N. (2014). Barriers for sustainable e-participation process: The case of Turkey. In *Government e-strategic planning and management* (pp. 227–243). New York, NY: Springer.

Kassen, M. (2015). *Understanding systems of e-government: e-Federalism and e-Centralism in the United States and Kazakhstan*. Lexington books.

Khan, G. F. (2015). The Government 2.0 utilization model and implementation scenarios. *Information Development, 31*(2), 135–149.

Kirillov, Z., Shmorgun, I., & Lamas, D. (2011, September). Towards the design of Estonia's m-government services. In *Proceedings of the 5th International Conference on Theory and Practice of Electronic Governance* (pp. 61–66). ACM.

Kitsing, M. (2008, May). Explaining the e-government success in Estonia. In *Proceedings of the 2008 International Conference on Digital Government Research* (pp. 429–430). Digital Government Society of North America.

Kitsing, M. (2011). Success without strategy: E-Government development in Estonia. *Policy & Internet, 3*(1), 1–21.

Klischewski, R. (2003). Top down or bottom up? How to establish a common ground for semantic interoperability within e-government communities. In *Proceedings of 1st International Workshop on E-Government at ICAIL E-Government: Modelling Norms and Concepts as Key Issues* (pp. 17–26).

Kotka, T., & Liiv, I. (2015, September). Concept of Estonian Government cloud and data embassies. In *International Conference on Electronic Government and the Information Systems Perspective* (pp. 149–162). Springer, Cham.

Kotka, T., Vargas, C. I., & Korjus, K. (2015). *Estonian e-Residency: Redefining the nation-state in the digital era. University of Oxford, Working Paper Series, 3*, 1–16.

Krimmer, R., Duenas-Cid, D., Krivonosova, I., Vinkel, P., & Koitmae, A. (2018, October). How much does an e-Vote cost? Cost comparison per vote in multichannel elections in Estonia. In *International Joint Conference on Electronic Voting* (pp. 117–131). Springer, Cham.

Krimmer, R., Triessnig, S., & Volkamer, M. (2007, October). The development of remote e-voting around the world: A review of roads and directions. In *International Conference on E-Voting and Identity* (pp. 1–15). Berlin, Heidelberg: Springer.

Krull, A. (2003). *ICT Infrastructure and E-readiness Assessment Report: Estonia* (Vol. 5). PRAXIS.

Kund, O., & Pau, A. (2018). New ID-card fault could have been intentional. *Postimees*. https://news.postimees.ee/4491312/new-id-card-fault-could-have-been-intentional. Accessed on: December 1, 2018.

Lathrop, D., & Ruma, L. (2010). *Open government: Collaboration, transparency, and participation in practice*. O'Reilly Media, Inc.

Layne, K., & Lee, J. (2001). Developing fully functional E-government: A four stage model. *Government Information Quarterly, 18*(2), 122–136.

Lee, M., Almirall, E., & Wareham, J. (2015). Open data and civic apps: First-generation failures, second-generation improvements. *Communications of the ACM, 59*(1), 82–89.

Lember, V., Kattel, R., & Tõnurist, P. (2018). Technological capacity in the public sector: The case of Estonia. *International Review of Administrative Sciences, 84*(2), 214–230.

Liiv, I. (2017). Welcome to E-Estonia, the tiny nation that's leading Europe in digital innovation. *The Conversation*, e7446.

Linders, D. (2012). From e-government to we-government: Defining a typology for citizen coproduction in the age of social media. *Government Information Quarterly, 29*(4), 446–454.

Loit, U., & Harro-Loit, H. (2012). Media policy in Estonia: Small market paradoxes. *Understanding Media Policies: A European Perspective, 85*.

Madise, Û., & Priit, V. (2011). Constitutionality of remote internet voting: The Estonian perspective. *Juridica Int'l, 18*, 4.

Martens, T. (2010). Electronic identity management in Estonia between market and state governance. *Identity in the Information Society, 3*(1), 213–233.

McBride, K., Matheus, R., Toots, M., Kalvet, T., & Krimmer, R. (2018, April). The role of linked open statistical data in public service co-creation. In *Proceedings of the 11th International Conference on Theory and Practice of Electronic Governance* (pp. 679–681). ACM.

MEAC. (2018). The Ministry of Economic Affairs and Communications. https://www.mkm.ee/en. Accessed on: November 24, 2018.

Meftah, M., Gharleghi, B., & Samadi, B. (2015). Adoption of E-government among Bahraini citizens. *Asian Social Science, 11*(4), 141.

Mergel, I. (2018). Open innovation in the public sector: Drivers and barriers for the adoption of Challenge. gov. *Public Management Review, 20*(5), 726–745.

Mergel, I., Kleibrink, A., & Sörvik, J. (2018). Open data outcomes: US cities between product and process innovation. *Government Information Quarterly*.

Moon, M. J., & Welch, E. W. (2005). Same bed, different dreams? A comparative analysis of citizen and bureaucrat perspectives on e-government. *Review of Public Personnel Administration, 25*(3), 243–264.

NENO. (2016). *The network of Estonian Nonprofit Organizations*. http://www.ngo.ee/neno. Accessed on: July 12, 2017.

NFCS. (2015). The National Foundation of Civil Society. www.kysk.ee/eng. Accessed on: January 25, 2016.

Nielsen, M. M. (2017, June). eGovernance and online service delivery in Estonia. In *Proceedings of the 18th Annual International Conference on Digital Government Research* (pp. 300–309). ACM.

Nielsen, M. M., & Krimmer, R. (2015, May). Reuse of data for personal and proactive service: An opportunity not yet utilised. In *CeDEM15: Conference for E-Democracy and Open Government* (Vol. 273). MV-Verlag.

ODC. (2018). *The Open Data Community*. www.opendata.ee.

ODP. (2015). *The Open Data Portal of Estonia*. https://opendata.riik.ee. Accessed on: May 30, 2016.

OECD. (2015). *OECD public governance reviews: Estonia and Finland: Fostering strategic capacity across government and digital services across borders*. OECD Publishing Paris.

OEF. (2015). *The open Estonia Foundation Project*. http://oef.org.ee/en/about-us. Accessed on: January 25, 2016.

OGP. (2012). *The open government partnership*. http://www.opengovpartnership.org/country/estonia. Accessed on: October 28, 2015.

OGP. (2015). *The open government partnership*. http://www.opengovpartnership.org/country/estonia. Accessed on: March 25, 2018.

Oll, M. (2015). *Estonia starts to export its budget visualization tool. The Estonian Public Broadcasting—ERR*. http://news.err.ee/v/scitech/982dd7f6-a769–43f7-b56b-318b26f485fd/estonia-starts-to-export-its-budget-visualization-tool. Accessed on: February 15, 2016.

Paide, K., Pappel, I., Vainsalu, H., & Draheim, D. (2018, April). On the systematic exploitation of the Estonian data exchange layer X-road for strengthening public-private partnerships. In *Proceedings of the 11th International Conference on Theory and Practice of Electronic Governance* (pp. 34–41). ACM.

Pappel, I., Pappel, I., Tepandi, J., & Draheim, D. (2017). Systematic digital signing in Estonian e-Government processes. In Transactions on large-scale data-and knowledge-centered systems XXXVI (pp. 31–51). Berlin, Heidelberg: Springer.

Peedu, G., & Lamas, D. (2011, September). Minu Viljandi: A case study on the effects of introducing web 2.0 features in e-government services on the overall user experience perception. In *Proceedings of the 5th International Conference on Theory and Practice of Electronic Governance* (pp. 305–308). ACM.

Polat, R. K. (2012). Digital exclusion in Turkey: A policy perspective. *Government Information Quarterly, 29*(4), 589–596.

Prause, G. (2016). E-Residency: A business platform for Industry 4.0? *Entrepreneurship and Sustainability Issues, 3*(3), 216–227.

Praxis. (2018). *The Praxis Think Tank*. http://www.praxis.ee/en. Accessed on: November 24, 2018.

Puussaar, A., Johnson, I. G., Montague, K., James, P., & Wright, P. (2018). Making open data work for civic advocacy. In *Proceedings of the ACM on Human-Computer Interaction, 2 (CSCW)*, 143.

Reporters Without Borders. (2018). https://rsf.org/en. Accessed on: October 2, 2018.

Robinson, N., & Martin, K. (2017). Distributed denial of government: The Estonian data embassy initiative. *Network Security, 2017*(9), 13–16.

Schnurer, E. B. (2015). E-Stonia and the future of the cyberstate. Foreign Affairs.
SEI (2015). The Stockholm Environment Institute. http://www.sei-international.org. Accessed on: July 12, 2017.
Smith, D. (2013b). *Estonia: Independence and European integration*. Routledge.
Soe, R. M., & Drechsler, W. (2018). Agile local governments: Experimentation before implementation. *Government Information Quarterly, 35*(2), 323–335.
Taagepera, R. (2018). *Estonia: Return to independence*. Routledge.
Tanel, K., & Sandra, S. (2015). Legal impediments in the EU to new technologies in the example of E-Residency. *Baltic Journal of Law & Politics, 8*(2), 71–90.
Tehnopol. (2018). *The technological business incubator*. http://www.tehnopol.ee/tehnopol/teaduspargist/?lang=en. Accessed on: November 24, 2018.
Temiz, S., & Brown, T. (2017). Open data project for e-government: Case study of Stockholm open data project. *International Journal of Electronic Governance, 9*(1–2), 55–84.
The community tools project. (2015). http://www.communitytools.info/en. Accessed on: December 25, 2015.
The Freedom House. (2018). https://freedomhouse.org/report/freedom-net/2018/estonia. Accessed on: October 2, 2018.
The Garage48 Project. (2018). http://garage48.org. Accessed on: December 1, 2018.
The Meieraha project. (2015). http://meieraha.eu/?lang=en. Accessed on: December 9, 2015.
The Office of the Kazakh Prime Minister. (2018). *Kazakh-Estonian forum: Bakytzhan Sagintayev invites Estonian business to active cooperation and implementation of joint projects*. https://primeminister.kz/en/news/all/17399. Accessed on: November 24, 2018.
The Public Information Act. (2000). https://www.riigiteataja.ee/en/eli/ee/Riigikogu/act/522122014002/consolide. Accessed on: November 24, 2018.
The Riigiraha project. (2015). http://riigiraha.fin.ee. Accessed on: November 18, 2015.
The Statistical Agency of Estonia. (2014). https://www.stat.ee. Accessed on: February 15, 2016.
The Valitsemise Valvurid Project. (2015). http://valvurid.err.ee. Accessed on: November 24, 2016.
Townsend, A. M. (2013). *Smart cities: Big data, civic hackers, and the quest for a new Utopia*. WW Norton & Company.
TUT. (2018). *The Tallinn University of Technology. The e-Governance technologies and services master's program*. http://www.egov.ee. Accessed on: October 2, 2018.
University of Tartu. (2015). *What happens to IT education in Estonia?* https://sisu.ut.ee/sites/default/files/what_happens_to_it_education_in_estonia_english.pdf. Accessed on: February 24, 2018.
UNPAN. (2018). *The global E-Government survey: Gearing E-Government to support transformation towards sustainable and resilient societies* https://publicadministration.un.org/egovkb/en-us/Reports/UN-E-Government-Survey-2018. Accessed on: November 18, 2018.
Vahtra-Hellat, A. (2015, February 17). 26 countries show interest in Estonia's e-state solutions. *The Estonian World*.
Varblane, U., & Varblane, U. (2018). The economic crisis and North Estonia: A case study of rapid recovery. In *Economic crisis and the resilience of regions*. Edward Elgar Publishing.
Vinkel, P., & Krimmer, R. (2016, October). The how and why to internet voting an attempt to explain E-Stonia. In *International Joint Conference on Electronic Voting* (pp. 178–191). Springer, Cham.
Wirtz, B. W., & Birkmeyer, S. (2015). Open government: Origin, development, and conceptual perspectives. *International Journal of Public Administration, 38*(5), 381–396.
Wirtz, B. W., Piehler, R., Thomas, M. J., & Daiser, P. (2016). Resistance of public personnel to open government: A cognitive theory view of implementation barriers towards open government data. *Public Management Review, 18*(9), 1335–1364.

Chapter 4
Open Data Politics in Kazakhstan: Understanding a Tentative Advance of Civic Engagement in a Transitional Society

4.1 Introduction. Open Data as a New Socioeconomic Phenomenon in Kazakhstan

Open data politics is a context-dependable phenomenon, especially when it comes to embracing strategies and tactics that policymakers and practitioners should adopt in order to achieve any progress in the area. After all, the political will of national authorities to promote open data platforms and the socioeconomic readiness of various stakeholders from private and non-governmental sectors to join the movement and contribute in a meaningful manner with their knowledge and assistance constitutes the very core of its implementation philosophy. In this respect, Kazakhstan could be regarded today as a real poster child of great socioeconomic opportunities that technology-driven reforms bring to public sector in a typical developing country, taking into account the impressive development of various e-commerce, e-banking, and e-government platforms in this emerging nation that have been recently noticed by experts from around the world and reflected in its overall progress in various global e-government ratings (UNPAN, 2003, 2004, 2005, 2008, 2010, 2012, 2014, 2016 and 2018).

The number one reason of the success in the area is that the implementation of e-government platforms has always been regarded as a matter of socioeconomic priority for national authorities, who usually regard any progress in the area as an important indicator of successful public sector reforms and overall technological development of the country. This, in turn, helps to increase its political image both domestically and, more importantly, internationally as an emerging digital state. Therefore, any achievements in building e-government in other countries are closely monitored, researched, and adopted by national authorities if they promise quick results, preferably in economic and social areas. In this regard, one of the most promising trends that are beginning to play an ever-increasing socioeconomic and potentially even political role today in the development of e-government in this Central Asian country is an open data movement. It is widely regarded by almost all

M. Kassen, *Open Data Politics*, SpringerBriefs in Political Science,
https://doi.org/10.1007/978-3-030-11410-7_4

stakeholders as a necessary prerequisite to reform a somewhat cumbersome and old public administration system that it had to inherit from the Soviet past almost three decades ago, especially in ensuring greater transparency of government in various public and semi-public institutions (i.e., a main target audience of open data politics is government itself), promoting e-participation trends among citizens (i.e., second audience are civic communities), and boosting public innovations in private and non-governmental sectors, especially among independent developers and businesses (third target audience). Advancing, respectively, administrative, social, and economic dimensions or pillars of open data politics (see Fig. 4.1), open data becomes, in fact, an intrinsic part of open government politics at all administrative levels (The Open Data Project of Kazakhstan, 2017).

In general, open data politics in Kazakhstan could be regarded as an integral part of the open government movement, which itself is apparently part of the e-government technological paradigm, taking into account the fact that they are both actively promoted by national authorities within a single unitary platform of digital government, often using the same digital ecosystem. Although the trend is slowly changing since some semi-public institutions are planning to initiate their own platforms in the area, the vast majority of datasets, regardless of whether they are representing national or local government agencies, are published through a single venue along with the traditional e-government ecosystem. Consequently, the concept is promoted in accordance with the same administrative logic, where the direct and very strict administrative commands or top-down directives play an important, if not crucial, role in its diffusion at all levels of government with its own advantages and disadvantages such as quite quick decision making at the expense

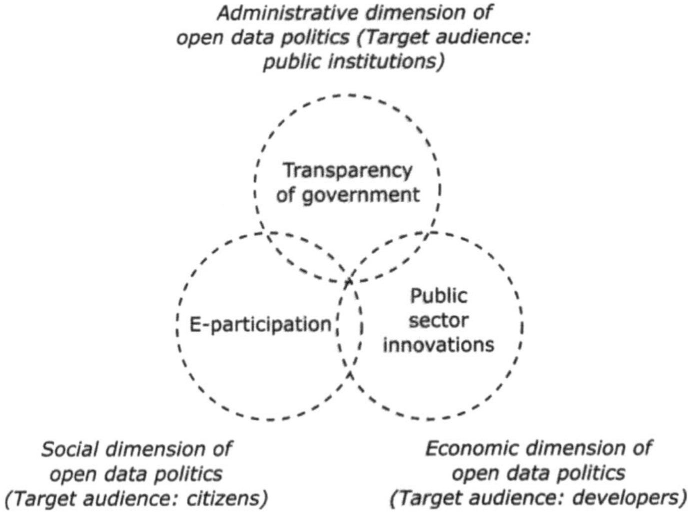

Fig. 4.1 Three pillars of open data politics in Kazakhstan. *Source* Own illustration

of a less collaborative dialogue between central and local authorities or between different institutional levels, taking into account the unitary structure of governance existing in this country.

In this regard, it seems interesting to understand how the concept of open data is perceived and, more importantly, realized in practice by policymakers and associated stakeholders such as e-government practitioners and state-owned telecommunication corporations that directly engaged in the implementation of all related projects in the area. Officially, the primary goal of the open data project is to increase the transparency of government agencies through the publication of public datasets in special depositories (The Open Data Project of Kazakhstan, 2017). Policymakers insist that the initiative could create a new channel of digital communication with business sectors and citizens, demonstrating the readiness of national authorities to be open to new progressive ideas. Probably, another indirect purpose of the project is to leverage a promising phenomenon of open data to accelerate the emergence of related e-participation, crowd-sourcing, and even civic engagement initiatives, including in an attempt to boost political image-making processes (Åström, Karlsson, Linde, & Pirannejad, 2012; Girish, Williams, & Yates, 2014), which, however, allows to leave intact fundamentals of old bureaucratic structures and post-totalitarian transitional mentality that continue to exist beyond quite successful digital or e-government realms. Therefore, any sophisticated public relations and extensive media campaigns play a significant role in the area, too, especially taking into account the fact that central government has always paid close attention to the promotion of national innovative projects among citizens and businesses in various media outlets and social networks, often even organizing various contests and competitions to attract new users and boost e-participation. This sui generis public relations policy later proved to be quite effective, generating new practical stories that could be interesting for open data policymakers and practitioners in other countries.

Another political goal of this policy is to demonstrate before both domestic and international audiences that e-government policymakers follow the universal trend that envisions open data as an essential part of the open government movement and try to implement the world's best practices in the area in an attempt to eventually improve its operation and, probably, rating in a global sense, since the operation of related projects, including national open data portals, is closely monitored today on a systematic basis by such global organizations as the United Nations (Stier, 2015), Open Government Partnership (Harrison, Pardo, & Cook, 2012), World Justice Project (WJP, 2017), and World Bank (Davies & Bawa, 2012). Therefore, any progress in the area could be indicative of the successful path that government official has chosen in all technology-driven public sector reforms. After all, Kazakhstan is a transitional society and many initiatives in the public sector are introduced in a tentative manner. Likewise, any potentially promising platforms that help to make public administration better and cost-effective, which are currently implemented at the national level, provide invaluable lessons to policymakers and practitioners in the area. In this respect, open data politics is an ideal playground to experiment with civic engagement and e-participation technologies, generating unique perspectives on the concept realization and resulting in some interesting findings, which are presented in this chapter.

4.2 The Context Analysis of the Open Data Movement

4.2.1 Understanding the Political Contexts

First, it is necessary to note that the promotion of e-government-related reforms has always been regarded as part of a much-greater project in Kazakhstan, namely the infrastructural and, more importantly, economic development of the country. To see this political trend, one should look at the history of e-government politics during the last two decades (Kassen, 2016), since almost all projects in the area have traditionally been accompanied with strong support and generous funding from the top political leadership. Actually, the introduction of e-government platforms in the early 2000s in a society that was not ready technologically to adopt the innovations, mostly because of low Internet penetration, computer literacy among the citizenry, and lack of infrastructure, has forced national authorities to invest heavily in all related areas. Informatization and computerization have been two watchwords that accompanied all e-government reforms in Kazakhstan. In this respect, the primary goal of open data politics is widely regarded by almost all public stakeholders as a matter of national socioeconomic priority.

Moreover, the government of Kazakhstan has some ambitions to enter the list of the 25 most developed countries in the world in terms of the e-government development (Information Kazakhstan—2020, 2013). The further promotion of open data platforms could play a key role in improving the overall position of the nation in the list. This, in turn, could be used later as a reference in political debates about the efficiency of national authorities in reforming public administration and the local economy. Therefore, any activity in this direction could be really rewarding and promising from this *sui generis* political perspective, guaranteeing a higher level of government attention to the topic and, more importantly, funding for the implementation of related public projects. In addition, the announced plans to ensure the constitutional transition of Kazakhstan from a strong presidential republic to a presidential-parliamentary system of governance could open new opportunities to promote civic engagement and participation in other branches of political power, too. These constitutional reforms, which were initiated by the presidential administration itself, send a strong political signal to promote more collaborative platforms of decision making in public institutions, including e-government-related areas.

4.2.2 *Understanding the Economic Contexts*

The economic environment has always played an important role in almost all public sector reforms in this transitional society, predetermining the implementation strategies and funding policies that e-government stakeholders have to choose in the area. Like in many parts of the world, citizens in Kazakhstan enjoy an explosive growth of information and communication technologies, whether it is in electronic commerce, social media activity, or various industries, which provide a robust technological basis to advance the open data concept in a wide range of sectors of economic activity. However, it is necessary to note that Kazakhstan has an economy which heavily relies on revenues from the extraction of mineral resources, first, oil, metals, and uranium, and currently suffers greatly from low commodity prices in global markets. The dramatic devaluation of the national currency since 2015 has allowed to partly ease the situation in the domestic market and remove the excessive burden on the national budget. But these fiscal measures have also caused hyperinflation domestically and forced authorities to cut many state programs and monitor closely any public spending, including in e-government areas. Therefore, the number priority is now to search for potentially more cost-effective solutions in the area, ideally with a minimum of investments from the public sector.

In this respect, the open data concept is widely regarded by local e-government stakeholders as an instrument that could potentially boost the business activity in the context of quite a lopsided economy due to the emergence of new start-ups and related market niches of mobile open data-driven applications and projects. In this case, government plays a role of a special platform or depositary that provides valuable information and datasets in a machine-readable format for various stakeholders from private and non-governmental sectors, first of all, developers, open data enthusiasts, and potential entrepreneurs who could boost business innovations in the area. For example, the vast majority of public awareness campaigns and public relations events in the areas such as various masters classes, conferences (Obi & Iwasaki, 2015), and forums, especially organized in partnership with foreign experts (OECD, 2016), which are all designed to promote the concept further, are mostly intended for local businesses and entrepreneurs so that they could create their own commercial products based on previously reused open data. Therefore, the project itself is aimed at developing an innovative economy in Kazakhstan that would less rely on lopsided and oil-dependent local economy. The current economic reality forces policymakers to improvise and resort to more cost-effective and pragmatic solutions in the area, including by adopting the best business models from foreign countries in e-government-related areas.

4.2.3 Understanding Social Contexts

When it comes to the implementation of open data policies, social context is a crucial factor of success. The knowledge that people have and opportunities that they could use to apply this knowledge are a recipe for the progress in the area. In this respect, it is necessary to note that Kazakhstan has almost all preconditions for the sustainable development of the concept, taking into account its decent socioeconomic indices (Trading Economics, 2017; World Bank, 2017). Literacy rate is one of the highest in the developing world (UNESCO, 2017). Many universities are experiencing an ever-increasing popularity of various non-humanitarian majors among students, especially in computer sciences, providing a steady flow of young professionals in the area to various sectors of national economy. The penetration of the Internet is also soaring across the country, and the number of users with high-speed access to the World Wide Web is steadily growing year by year (see Table 4.1). All these conditions create a truly favorable socioeconomic basis to promote open data policies, which, as a rule, require a developed human capital since the realization of the concept is all about networking and collaboration.

In this respect, the open data concept could also be regarded as quite an effective tool to boost the professional development of local computer specialists by increasing their competence and expertise in open data. The ultimate goal is to outsource in the foreseeable future some of the public services to the private sector, i.e., finding new more sustainable ways to save public funds and human resources. This could be achieved by resorting to a really powerful tool of the collective wisdom of civil society and decreasing the operational costs of various public administration systems due to civic engagement and collaboration from the part of various independent developers, businesses, and non-governmental organizations. These stakeholders could cooperate in co-financing various collaborative platforms and initiatives in the area. The promotion of open data-driven projects in private and non-governmental sectors could potentially create a new lucrative source to

Table 4.1 The Internet penetration in Kazakhstan in 2009–2016

Year	Internet users	Penetration (% of total population) (%)	Total population	Non-users (Internetless)
2016	9,961,519	55.80	17,855,384	176,681
2015	9,784,837	55.50	17,625,226	249,555
2014	9,535,283	54.90	17,371,621	301,528
2013	9,233,755	54	17,099,546	265,284
2012	8,968,471	53.30	16,821,455	591,993
2011	8,376,478	50.60	16,554,305	3,222,321
2010	5,154,157	31.60	16,310,624	2,224,256
2009	2,929,901	18.20	16,098,356	1,179,145

Source Elaboration based on sample data from Internet Live Stats (2017b)

generate various digital services for citizens and businesses, providing a certain second market to advance independent e-government solutions and related networking start-ups in the area.

4.2.4 Understanding the International Contexts

The global publicity plays an important role in e-government politics, too, taking into account that often information on the independent observation and review of various digital projects and platforms could be obtained only with the help of the international community as cross-border comparison really matters. Therefore, the related activity of the United Nations, World Bank, and Open Government Partnership in the area has recently helped to create a strong global community of independent experts who could provide a systematic analysis and, more importantly, assessment of individual nations in the area. The generation of various rankings and ratings in such areas of technology-driven public sector reforms as e-government, e-commerce, e-participation, open legislation, open data, etc. creates a wholesome atmosphere of competition, co-creation, and sharing among various nations. In this regard, it is necessary to note that the implementation of open data strategies plays an important role as an economic tool to improve public administration and advance public sector innovations thanks to citizen or crowd-sourcing. Moreover, it also offers an indirect political instrument to boost the image of the whole e-government idea both domestically and internationally.

In the case of Kazakhstan, the implementation of digital policies in the area is widely considered as an additional channel to promote public relations in related public debates. The advance of the open data concept is regarded by policymakers today as a new great opportunity to globally boost the positive image of the country as a technologically modern nation. Indeed, this distinctive policy of global publicity in the e-government area has proved to be very effective in recent years; especially, when it comes to efforts in promoting the country in various related rating lists, one of the most notorious of which is a biennial global ranking carried out and published by the United Nations Public Administration Network (UNPAN). As a result, the steady progress of the nation in creating various e-government and e-commerce platforms, including with the help of various open data-driven solutions, is one of the most important factors in building digital society and, more importantly, developed economy, which could lead to positive outcomes for the whole society. Technological achievements in the area could also significantly improve the business climate in a digital manner and positively affect the investment status of the nation.

4.3 The Analysis of Open Data Regulation

The realization of the open data concept is a quite specific aspect of government activity, which requires special regulations and legal procedures in order to ensure a steady generation of government datasets and, more importantly, their publication in the area. It is especially important to find a right balance between ensuring a systematic and quick update of all datasets on the one hand and guaranteeing the right of people to keep secret their personal information or confidential details on the other hand. Personal information as well as state and commercial secrets could be accidentally published as part of open data in a bureaucratic environment where public servants could be administratively forced to expedite the publication of government datasets in their particular areas of activity due to some subjective or objective reasons. Law is the only document that should regulate such activities. In this respect, it is necessary to note that in Kazakhstan legally the public access to government information, including to open data, is regulated today by three fundamental documents, in particular, by the Article 18 of the Constitution of the country that guarantees the right of citizens to access government information (The Constitution of Kazakhstan, 1998), by the data privacy law that aims to protect an unauthorized publication of personal data (Law # 94-V, 2013), and by the special freedom of information law that in the Article 10 explicitly requires all government agencies to publish their datasets in a proactive manner in special public digital depositories (Law # 401-V, 2015). The three documents provide, respectively, political, technological, and administrative dimensions for the regulation of the open data movement in Kazakhstan (see Fig. 4.2).

It is interesting to note that the American tradition of the freedom of information acts (FOIA) or its European analogue—the access to information laws—adopted a few decades ago in the USA (Katz, 1969; Wald, 1984) and many countries of the European Union (Ackerman & Sandoval-Ballesteros, 2006; Banisar, 2004) to legally regulate the sphere has been an unknown practice in Kazakhstan until recently. The Kazakh Law on Access to Information was finally adopted only in November 2015 (The Strategy 2050, 2015) after really long and intense debates and discussions between central government on the one hand and various domestic and, more importantly, international intergovernmental and non-governmental organizations on the other (LPRC, 2015), especially over the legal details of such regulation. For example, some drafts of the first versions of the FOIA have been previously developed and discussed with active participation of the Office for Democratic Institutions and Human Rights under the auspices of the Organization for Security and Cooperation in Europe (OSCE, 2015). In this respect, the adoption of the law provides a powerful legal instrument to promote the concept at the national level and sends an indirect political signal to all potential stakeholders to join the open data movement. The document unambiguously endorses the reuse of government datasets by third parties, potentially decreasing dramatically the

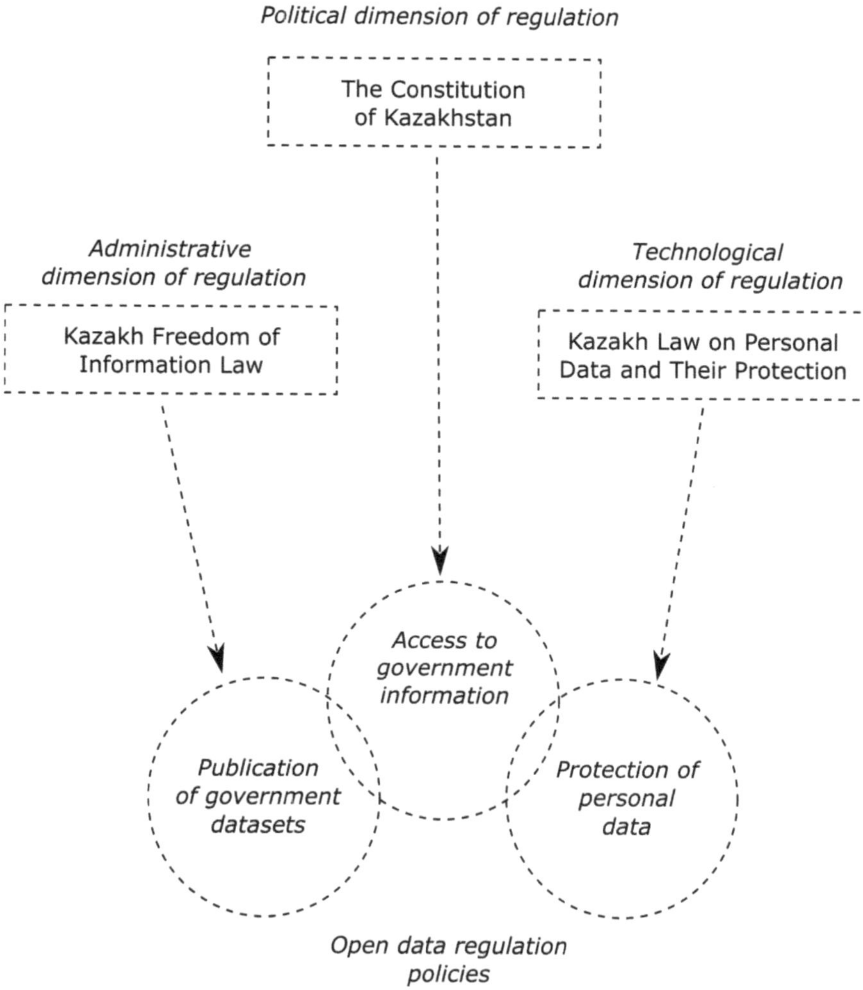

Fig. 4.2 The open data regulation policies in Kazakhstan. *Source* Own illustration

traditional monopoly of the state in the area. Moreover, the document creates a robust legal basis for all government and semi-public institutions to be more active in publishing their datasets through the single portal of open data.

4.4 The Networking Analysis of the Open Data Stakeholders in Kazakhstan

The specifics of open data politics imply an active stance of various stakeholders in promoting a wide range of activities and related collaborative and, more importantly, networking start-ups and projects, which are usually initiated and created by independent players in the area. In this regard, it is necessary to identify who the key stakeholders of open data politics are and understand what roles they play in related networking activities. It is interesting to note that the Kazakh platform of open data explicitly identifies several target audiences that could directly benefit from the implementation of the project (The Open Data Project of Kazakhstan, 2017) such as *government agencies* (e.g., in saving budget funds due to the utilization of related citizen-sourcing tools and engagement of the private sector and developers to share new ideas on how to improve together the work of various digital public sector platforms and systems), *non-governmental organizations* (e.g., in enjoying a fundamental right to scrutinize the activity of government agencies and related technology-driven public sector reforms), *citizens* (e.g., in making the community life in their neighborhoods better and safer), *businesses* (e.g., in improving various information and interactive e-commerce services), and, more importantly, *independent ICT developers* (e.g., in generating new ideas on how to promote various collaborative start-ups, hackathons, and networking initiatives in the e-government area for citizens and businesses).

4.4.1 Understanding the Role of Public Agencies

The public sector is a key player in open data politics in Kazakhstan. In this respect, the implementation of the concept is regarded as an element of public sector reforms which could boost civic engagement and e-participation and potentially enrich the e-government ecosystem with new more collaborative domains of interaction with other stakeholders, first of all, independent developers, businesses, and non-governmental organizations. Therefore, any progress in the area is welcomed and strongly supported by the government as it facilitates networking and exchanges of knowledge in the area. Taking into account the fact that almost all information pertaining to government activities is generated and stored by public agencies themselves, the central government of Kazakhstan plays a crucial role in promoting the open data concept at all institutional levels. Moreover, being regarded technologically as an intrinsic part of the e-government ecosystem, the open data project is deemed to be aimed at not only popularizing related political and ideological aspects of the open government concept among all members of civil society such as the promotion of direct communication with public agencies and participation in related decision-making platforms but also fostering economic development of the country due to greater citizen-sourcing and funding in the area.

In this respect, the Ministry of Investments and Development (MID, 2016) provides a political supervision over the development of both open data projects and almost all e-government platforms through specialized semi-public agencies and state-owned companies, which themselves follow a traditional logic of the double-layer bureaucratic subordination and administrative control. Such organizations as the National Agency for Technological Development (NATD, 2016), the National Information Technologies Agency (NIT, 2016), and Infocommunication

Development Fund (ICT Fund, 2016), which play a crucial role in the development of all public technology-driven projects at the national level, are all organizationally controlled today by the Kazakh National Infocommunication Holding (Zerde, 2015). Despite their semi-private status, all these agencies have always had access to ample funding and resorted to the traditional top-down mechanisms of the e-government development. In this regard, the policymakers have quickly realized that this combination of administrative control and direct funding from the national budget could be a highly effective tool to advance open data, too. Therefore, almost all measures to diffuse the concept across various public agencies have been promoted via traditional administrative directives. Although the same trend could be traced today almost in any unitary country, Kazakhstan is unique in a sense that it fully enjoys the lack of external partisan control from the political opposition in the area, which could otherwise have provided an additional layer of scrutiny, political control, and public monitoring. As a result, the overwhelming role of government institutions and affiliated semi-public structures allows to expedite the implementation of related reforms in a favorable context of administrative centralization.

4.4.2 Understanding the Role of Independent Developers

The socioeconomic role of independent developers in promoting the open data movement is difficult to overestimate since their direct participation in reusing and processing further various government datasets constitutes a core of the concept implementation philosophy. *If open government data is just a material, raw and unsystematized, then developers are masters, who could create something useful for the general public from these huge massive stockpiles of information.* In this respect, taking into account the fact that today the promotion of any civic engagement and collaborative projects in the e-governance areas, especially related to the promotion of open data phenomena, is unimaginable without direct involvement and networking of independent developers, their political will to join the movement and boost the mutually beneficial cooperation with government agencies in creating various open data-driven projects is especially important. In fact, the independent networks of Kazakh developers play a critical role, to some extent, of a technological bridge between government and citizens, i.e., a proxy that makes the concept more or less sustainable as a truly collaborative public project. Indeed, if e-government platforms publish datasets in machine-readable formats that need some technological processing as a raw material, which could be often provided only by an army of computer designers, coders, programmers, testers, and various open data entrepreneurs from the business sector and non-governmental organizations and even sometimes with the participation of technically savvy citizens and students of technological universities, their socioeconomic readiness to cooperate with the public sector in creating third-party open data-driven start-ups is a crucial element in promoting the open data concept as a sustainable collaborative philosophy.

The communication in social media networks, the launch of various public relations campaigns, and the organization of technological contests and hackathons are the most effective ways to promote the idea of open data. For example, social media plays a very important role as a certain platform for open professional cooperation in the area among various stakeholders, not only those who call themselves independent developers but also professionals and e-government experts from various public agencies and national telecommunication corporations. Various accounts of ICT specialists in such popular global networking platforms as Facebook, Twitter, Vkontakte, Bitbucket, and Github as well as frequent organization of various hackathons or app contests, e.g., the HackDay Kazakhstan (HDK, 2015), MOST hackathons (MOST, 2017), and forums of e-government experts such as the Ted^{x}Astana (The Tedxastana Project, 2015), the Week of Innovations (Kazinform, 2015), and the TechConnect and Open Data Conference (The Techconnect Project, 2015) are the most interesting venues to promote such networking platforms among Kazakh professionals in the computer field. The organization of these networking events also opens new opportunities to engage various business players to the movement both domestically and internationally. For example, such transnational corporations as Microsoft and Samsung actively participate in organizing related contests for a wide community of local developers and independent experts in the area (The Electronic Government of Kazakhstan, 2017; Yvision, 2011). The government officials in cooperation with the private sector often help developers to launch online contests and organize master classes and special open lunches. The special format of meetings, which are often called as brown bag seminars, helps programmers, experts, and designers meet in person, network and brainstorm new ideas. In an environment of open discussion, they project new open data-driven applications, develop better interfaces for existing mobile platforms, and initiate collaborative start-ups. One of the most promising platforms for such cooperation is offered by the Astana International IT and Startup Hub (AIITSH, 2018). The ultimate goal of public–private partnerships in the area is to generate expertise and create new digital services for citizens and businesses (see Fig. 4.3).

4.4.3 Understanding the Role of the Non-governmental Sector

It is necessary to note that the consultative and methodological assistance of various international and domestic non-governmental players provides an additional channel of support to promote the open data movement in Kazakhstan. The promotion of the concept among public agencies and increasing popularity of related open data-driven projects launched independently by a wide community of developers and technically savvy citizens attract the attention of various foreign non-governmental and nonprofit organizations to the phenomena, which they see as

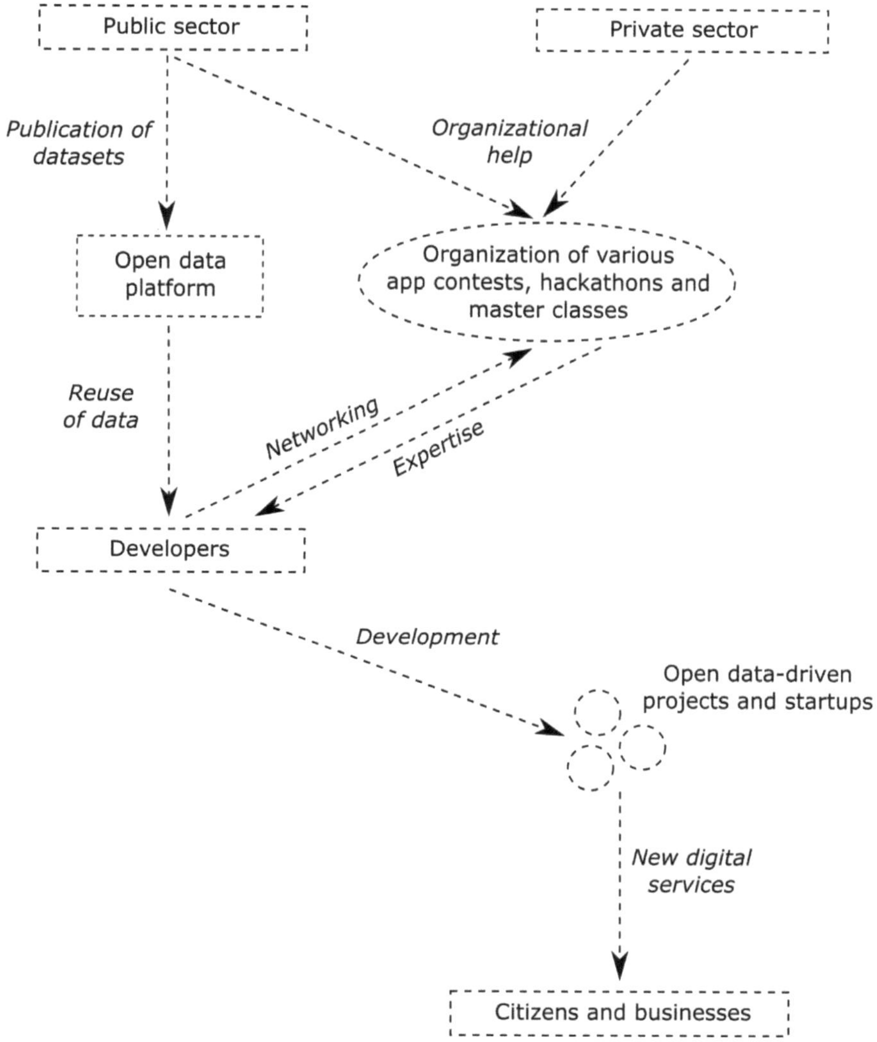

Fig. 4.3 The role of public–private partnerships in open data politics in Kazakhstan. *Source* Own illustration

a certain experimental platform to test the socioeconomic and even political implications of the concept in an unusual cultural context, indirectly experimenting with potential e-democracy platforms in the region. For example, such globally renowned non-governmental actor in the e-government area as the Center for Open Data Enterprise, an international expert venue specializing on open data research and consultations, provides valuable advisory and technical assistance to the open data projects in Kazakhstan, especially in organizing various roundtables, master classes, and participating in global exchange of knowledge (The Electronic

Government of Kazakhstan, 2015). They have helped to organize recently a number of meetings for local developers in close partnership with experts from the Open Data 500, an international network of ICT organizations created by the Government Lab Project in the New York University that studies the impact of the open data concept on the advance of democracy and civil society at the global level (The Open Data 500 Global Network, 2015). In this regard, the public–private partnership in the area has helped to ensure the overall sustainability of the open data concept as a truly multidimensional international collaborative project, when all three key stakeholders of the open data movement in Kazakhstan are equally interested in the mutually beneficial cooperation in the area, since *public sector* regards it as a great opportunity to demonstrate transparency in government, *developers* enjoy new unprecedented opportunities to play with various ICT-driven platforms, and finally, *global* and *domestic non-governmental organizations* envision a potentially promising playground to experiment with various e-democracy technologies and platforms in an unusual context of transitional economy and post-totalitarian society.

4.5 The Policy Review of Government Strategies in the Area

4.5.1 Promoting Centralized Publication of Datasets

One of the most important elements of open data politics is the publication of government datasets itself through the official portal of open data by various ministries, departments, and, in some cases, even semi-public agencies and state-owned companies and corporations. In this respect, policymakers have adopted a very cost-effective way to promote the concept in Kazakhstan in accordance with the established mechanisms of public administration and administrative traditions of decision making since almost all datasets in the area are aggregated by central government itself from a massive database of information, documents, files, and charts that were previously generated by various agencies, whether they are ministries, departments, akimats (municipalities in Kazakh), etc. through a wide network of intra-governmental networks and internal channels of communication. The introduction of electronic document flow systems in the early 2000s helped to significantly simplify the process of generation and automatic analysis in the area, resulting in quite a systematic update of the national open data platform. For example, by the end of March 2017, the portal has published more than 2000 datasets distributed among such categories as international relations, employment, education, transport and communication, legal assistance, culture, social welfare, taxation and finances, citizenship and migration, social security and healthcare, local government, trade, etc.

Technologically, the public release of government datasets is an absolutely new phenomenon in Kazakhstan and all organizational aspects of these activities are regulated not only by traditional regulatory documents such as FOIA and information security laws but also by various executive ordinances and resolutions that could be adopted at different institutional levels if necessary. In general, according to the law on access to information (Law # 401-V, 2015), only data that is regarded as public could be published by government agencies. In this regard, the datasets usually contain such types of information on public institutions as descriptions of services, statistical data, contact details of public agencies, geotags, etc. which help developers to create a diverse range of open data-driven products, e.g., visualization and mapping tools as well as various marketing and research instruments intended for use in both desktop and mobile platforms. Officially, the open data portal was initiated in 2013 and at early stages of its development was regarded as a playground for e-government policymakers to see the socioeconomic potential of the projects, publishing only a few hundreds of datasets annually. In this respect, the adoption of the Kazakh FOIA at the end of 2015 provided a robust legal basis for government institutions to boost the publication of various datasets in the area and sent a strong political signal to all stakeholders to join the movement, resulting in an explosive generation of datasets.

4.5.2 *Promoting an Interactive and Collaborative Update of Datasets*

It is interesting to note that e-government policymakers also adopted a popular strategy in implementing various technological aspects of open data politics by paying special attention to the collaborative solutions in promoting the national platform in the area. For example, citizens and businesses could send their personalized requests to government agencies through the single e-government ecosystem to publish datasets that are currently not included in the list, providing quite an effective instrument to ensure greater participation from the part of all interested in stakeholders. Moreover, in order to provide developers with a more sophisticated instrument of software development for their open data-driven projects and start-ups, technologically, this ecosystem also allows both offline (manual) and interactive update of datasets in mobile applications. This technological measure, in turn, has a positive effect on the overall sustainability of open data-driven projects and start-ups in the future. Most of them are usually created by independent developers and technically savvy citizens who tend to minimize time and resources invested into the projects and often are not ready to maintain them later in a more systematic manner if it is not possible to automate at least partly some of the functions. It is especially true when the open data-driven projects are handed over to third parties, e.g., non-governmental organizations and individual citizens, who are usually more interested in continuing the concept only if it requires basic technical maintenance and results in low operation costs. Volunteers could be very enthusiastic in joining the movement, too, but their contribution could be really modest or useless if there is no technological means to harness the potential of civic engagement in these projects.

In this regard, the initial investment of time, common sense, and expertise in the development of sustainable mechanisms in promoting the concept seems to be one of the most important steps in this technological process. The practical opportunity to easily modify the interface of the software and use interactive functions (e.g., the automated update of datasets and options to use distant technical support that could be initially embedded by independent developers in the layout and source codes of open data-driven projects) could dramatically increase later the number of volunteers who would be inspired by this technology and continue the projects, paying less attention to the manual and quite mundane update and maintenance of such projects. Therefore, the will of local developers and technically savvy citizens to invest their time and resources to open data start-ups, often on a charitable basis, is a crucial factor of success in the area. Original software designers play an important role not only in the development of the projects at the beginning of their technological life cycles but also in further diffusion of the whole concept among other stakeholders such as non-governmental organizations, businesses, and citizens. After all, any promotion of open data politics in the future could be ineffective if there is no interactive feedback between those who publish government datasets on the one hand and those who reuse them in their projects on the other. It is necessary to understand that the mutually beneficial nature of the concept could be harnessed only with the help of all interested stakeholders. Therefore, independent developers are a bridge or proxy, whose participation, at first glance, may seem invisible yet, as it turned out, very important for the sustainable development of the concept.

4.5.3 Promoting the Single Ecosystem of Digital Government

Although the concept of open data is at its infancy in Kazakhstan, the official project itself is promoted strategically and maintained technologically in accordance with a traditional model of implementation derived from an administrative practice that has been previously developed and widely used in advancing almost all e-government public sector reforms. Same as in Estonia, the Kazakh model of open government politics, which embraces a strictly centralized approach in governance and does not differentiate at all any distinction between local and national open data projects, represents a typical unitary approach in building-related open data projects. Again, all datasets are published through a single channel of distribution and publication at the national digital government portal—data.egov.kz. In this regard, in contrast to e-centralism, the federal model of the e-government implementation in the USA or *e-federalism,* which could be characterized by a really strict and unambiguous political division between national, state, and local open data platforms, has been later practically evolved into its more sophisticated and conceptually continuous paradigm at the confederal level in the European Union. The paradoxical coexistence of various regional, national, and local e-government platforms there with supranational open data platforms such as the Open Data Europe (ODE, 2016), the European Data Platform (EDP, 2017), and the Public Data Platform (PDP, 2017) could be tentatively called as *an electronic confederalism* or *e-confederalism* (Kassen, 2018). This implementation strategy apparently propagates a much-greater administrative autonomy and discretion of national authorities in decision making in related e-government reforms in Europe, especially at different institutional echelons of government and equally at different regional and local levels of power.

It is interesting to note that in Kazakhstan, the implementation of the open data project is carried out within the same e-government ecosystem, where traditional digital services and government datasets are provided through a single platform. Public agencies equally at national, provincial, and local levels of government generate, aggregate, and publish their datasets in a centralized manner. In this respect, citizens and businesses could use them for their own purposes, e.g., monitoring government activities, using in research and statistics or for marketing purposes, while *independent developers* could reuse them to create open data-driven projects and start-ups, providing a new source of digital services for people (see Fig. 4.4). In this respect, the automatic aggregation and integration of open data from all public agencies in one digital venue helps to ensure a single authorization policy in the area, the policy that reflects well the unitary structure of the nation, where many official technology-driven initiatives and projects in the e-government area are traditionally advocated and financially supported by the government at the national level. As a result, e-centralism or the unitary model of e-government implementation allows national authorities to expedite the launch of various projects in the area. Along with single public funding and single legislation in the area, it gives the central government a very powerful instrument of administrative control over the promotion of open data initiatives at all levels of power.

4.5.4 Promoting Feedback Options and Public Awareness Campaigns in the Area

When it comes to technology-driven public sector reforms, publicity really matters. It is all the more so in the open data area. It is especially important to boost public relations campaigns among developers, businesses, and technically savvy citizens,

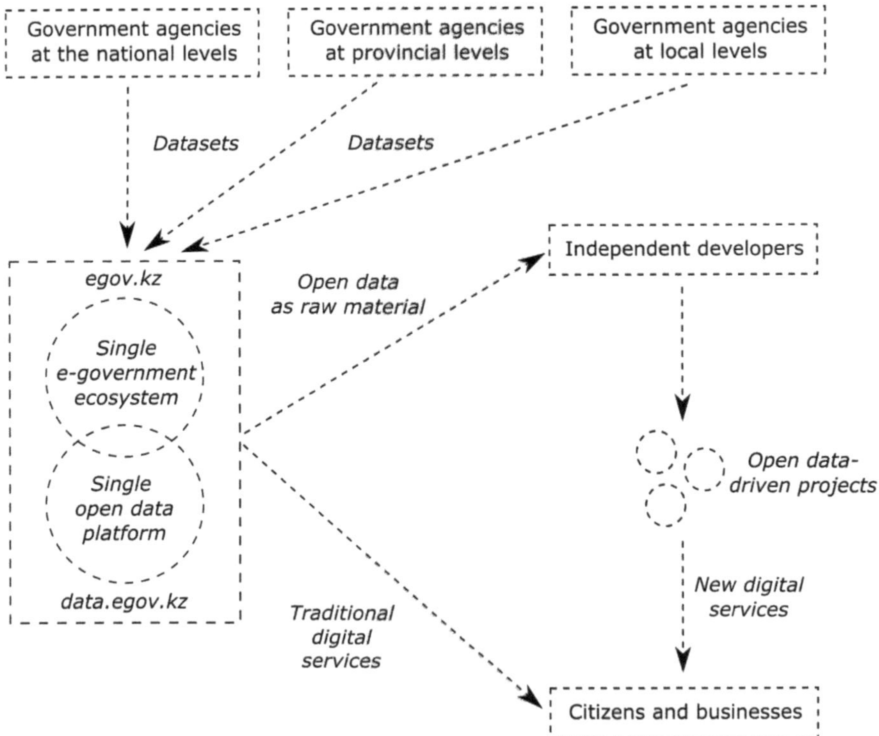

Fig. 4.4 E-centralism as a strategy in promoting open data politics in Kazakhstan. *Source* Own illustration

whose participation in related activities, e.g., in reusing government datasets and creating various open data-driven projects and commercial and collaborative start-ups, is a concrete indicator of progress and any achievements in the area should be monitored and, if necessary, rewarded by officials. In this respect, one of the most remarkable features in the development of the national open data platform in Kazakhstan is the provision of various feedback options that welcome reaction from all interested stakeholders in an attempt to leverage a promising phenomenon of civic engagement. The ultimate technological goal of the strategy is to make the interface of the system better, more intuitive, and user-centered. Moreover, it provides some user guidance and video materials for potential developers in the area on how to use government datasets, explaining in detail the implementation process and even learning on how to code some basic applications, computer programs, and mashups, which could be used later by everyone in generating new ideas, proposals, and start-ups aimed at improving related projects.

Moreover, e-government policymakers have resorted to a number of popular publicity platforms and media campaigns in the area, which are intrinsically aimed at a wide community of Kazakh developers and students in various technological universities and colleges. For example, in order to facilitate the growth of civic engagement and collaboration around the national open data project, its administrators have recently organized a wide range of master classes, prize contests, and professional competitions such as the e-Government Hackathons (Manley, 2015), the Startup Battles Project (SBP, 2016), or multiple and widespread open data hack days at local levels. Another aspect of public awareness campaigns is the promotion of various networking activities in the area as well as a number of community platforms and events such as The Tech Garden Project (TGP, 2016) and The Innovation Week (Kazakh, 2015) among various independent Kazakh developers, professional coders, designers and, more importantly, business persons and non-governmental organizations. In general, the organization of such contests among professional networks of e-government, open data experts, and e-commerce experts helps to identify the most urgent community needs and challenges and dramatically broadens the pool of potential stakeholders and contributors for the open data-driven ecosystem in Kazakhstan.

4.6 The Content Analysis of the Open Data-Driven Projects

The analysis of independent open data-driven projects is probably one of the most important aspects in evaluating the overall realization of the concept in one particular country. Although, officially, the open data portal in Kazakhstan was launched in 2013, its operation as a single provider of various government datasets has already led to the creation of a number of interesting third-party open data-driven projects, mostly, at the national level. The projects claim to be independent and rely on the promise of civic engagement and active participation of the members of civil society. However, it is necessary to note that the administrators of the official open data project try to track the further reuse of government datasets in the private sector and even publish all information related to third-party open data-driven initiatives on their single portal with a short description of the start-ups, the full names of their developers, and even hyperlinks to the installation distributives. In this regard, the distributives could be downloaded from the App Store or Google Play accounts.

4.6.1 The Healthcare Project: Raising Public Awareness About Free Medical Services

One of the most interesting open data-driven initiatives created independently by developers in Kazakhstan is the Healthcare project (HCP, 2017), which allows citizens to find all information, consultations, and advice on topics associated with the provision of healthcare and medical products. For example, the mobile application, which distributives could be freely downloaded from the App Store, publishes the list of organizations and institutions where citizens and legal residents of Kazakhstan could receive free medical services and medicaments that are guaranteed by the local social security act. It also updates, in an interactive mode, the current list of illnesses which could be treated in foreign hospitals at the expense of budgetary funds with the indication of all addresses, names, and telephones of related medical organizations and legal documents that provide a regulatory basis for the provision of such support from government (see Fig. 4.5). The emergence of the project that uses open data from the official open government portal seems especially timely since at the moment the national authorities are initiating a universal healthcare plan that would cover the whole population of the country, regardless of whether it is in urban areas and countryside. The initiatives could be especially interesting for low-income citizens and underrepresented communities throughout the nation.

4.6.2 The Business Registration Checker: Promoting Open Data-Driven Services for Business Communities

Another interesting open data-driven initiative is the business registration checker project (BRC, 2017), which was created on the basis of datasets from the Kazakh internal revenue service and state registry of legal entities and enterprises and is specifically designed to help small businesses and individual entrepreneurs to see all registration credentials and documents of their business clients and service providers in an interactive and anonymous manner. Ideally, the platform could be used by business people in order to check potential partners for any fraudulent activities and violations of business etiquettes that they could have had previously in the market. Such information could be especially interesting for representatives of semi-public and private organizations that are directly engaged in the organization of public procurement operations for government agencies and affiliated structures since they are obliged to guarantee the high quality of their services. Many of the services are rendered in partnership with various contractors and subcontractors from the private sector, and the centralized database which would allow users to quickly obtain general information about legal entities they are dealing with is in high demand in the market today. Another potential target audience for the project is a wide community of foreign investors whose potential will to cooperate with local business partners in the area in a mutually beneficial manner could be hindered by the lack of knowledge about these local business entities.

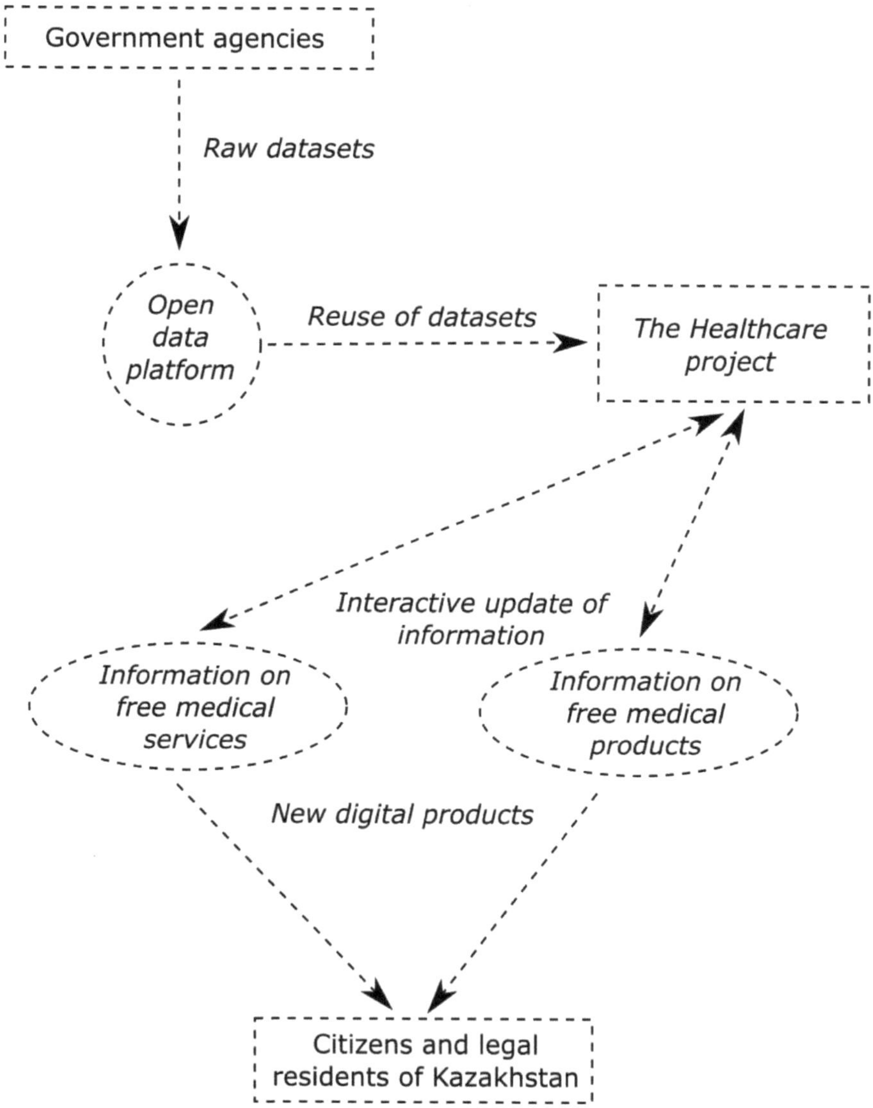

Fig. 4.5 Raising public awareness about the universal healthcare system in Kazakhstan. *Source* Own illustration

4.6.3 The TengeApp Project: Promoting Financial and Economic Information

One more independent start-up that reuses open data from public platforms in Kazakhstan is the TengeApp initiative. This open data-driven app is a classical example of a mashup, i.e., a special computer program or mobile application that aggregates information and data from different sources and platforms both public and private to create new digital services and products. In this respect, the app provides a wide range of information services for citizens such as data on current exchange rates of foreign currencies in Kazakhstan (TAP, 2017). Taking into account the fact that foreign import closes the shortages for the vast majority of goods and products in the market, the financial system of the country suffers greatly from the extreme dollarization of local economy, which directly affects many spheres and niches of human activity in this country, and this mobile application is in high demand among small and medium businesses, which need to know the latest rates in order to stay afloat. In addition, it also provides some financial data from the Kazakh Stock Exchange Market, quotations of commodities, basic economic indicators of the country, socioeconomic statistics, etc. The app was designed, first of all, for business persons, bankers, traders, entrepreneurs, journalists, researchers, and all those who are interested in receiving the latest information on the financial and economic development of the country.

4.7 Discussion: Locating the Key Challenges of the Open Data Movement in Kazakhstan

4.7.1 The Paradoxical Lack of Open Data-Driven Projects in the Political Domain

The promotion of open data policies could potentially boost both political and economic development of nations that adopted related implementation strategies and organizational tactics in fulfilling public sector reforms, especially if they allow to dramatically advance the key public values and benefits of the concept such as civic engagement, e-participation, collaboration, and public sector innovations. In this respect, one of the most interesting aspects that one can notice in the development of open data-driven projects in Kazakhstan is a lack of initiatives that are aimed at promoting civic engagement and increased collaboration exclusively in the political domain of the concept such as projects that propagate greater transparency of government institutions through independent open data-driven platforms. Through these third-party projects, citizens could have directly participated in decision-making processes, tracked better lobbying activity, contributed more to the lawmaking processes, etc. even if they already have the opportunity to take part and input personally or collectively in various similar promising projects, which are administered today within the national e-government project. However, despite the efforts of the central government to promote equally the open data phenomena in all dimensions of the concept, regardless of whether they are in economic, social, or political ones, the primary focus of independent open data-driven projects on the development of socioeconomic aspects is apparent. The trend is a consequence of the recent ubiquitous tradition to value the economic aspects of public sector reforms over the political ones in multiple programs that the government has been carrying out for the last two decades. Any developments aimed at political transformations have been usually regarded as quite sensitive in the area and, therefore, often avoided by developers and open data enthusiasts in their third-party collaborative projects. As a result, the socioeconomic dimension of the concept promotion is a realm where a vast majority of related open data-driven start-ups are being advanced at the moment.

Policy recommendation

The presence of positive political signals and greater publicity in the area of open data could help to promote the concept further. In this connection, the recent adoption of the national law on access to information, i.e., of the Kazakh version of FOIA, sends a certain political signal to all stakeholders, especially independent developers, businesses, and non-governmental organizations to join the open data movement and harness the public value of the concept in an attempt to boost the development of the nation, hopefully, both economically and politically. In this respect, it is very important to initiate extensive media and publicity campaigns among various stakeholders, especially non-governmental organizations and independent activists so that they would join the movement and contribute with new ideas on how to advance more in the political dimension of the open data movement. The advocacy of public relations campaigns among various independent developers and technically savvy citizens, calling them to pay special attention to the development of open data-driven projects that would be aimed at increasing government transparency and accountability, should be a promising starting point for various lobbying activities in the area. This could also be a motivation for political groups to engage in the movement and contribute ideologically through debates and discussion. Collaboration is a key ingredient of the successful formulae for any progress in the area.

4.7.2 Decision Making and Discretion Really Matters

Some may think that the publication of open data is a trivial administrative process since it usually implies, at first glance, a simple generation of government datasets, their systematization, selection, and, finally, publication in special digital depositories. After all, computerization has greatly simplified such process of publication. In this regard, the adoption of the law on access to information in late 2015 paved the direct way to a more systematic publication of government datasets in special digital depositories. According to e-government policymakers, in general, up to 70% of government information could be published online as open data today in Kazakhstan (Orazgaliyeva, 2015). But not all information could be stored openly in the Internet due to some reasons. For example, some data is really challenging to publicize in a computer-readable format due to a simple fact that it only exists as a paper document or these files may contain some personal and commercial data or other types of confidential information, which should not be published according to the existing laws. In addition, even if such information or data could be disclosed by law, the level of discretion by public servants and administrators in decision making in the area at the moment could be extremely limited or even non-existent not only due to ubiquitous bureaucracy and red tape that still exists in many public institutions but also due to the lack of traditions of self-regulation, administrative autonomy, and lack of competence and technical knowledge. After all, the realization of open data philosophy is, to a greater degree, a context-dependable undertaking, where the traditions of government transparency, discretion in public administration, and socioeconomic readiness of both administrators and citizens are crucial factors of success.

Policy recommendation

One of the possible solutions to address the challenge could be found in the reformation of public sector itself, especially in providing greater autonomy and administrative discretion in related decision-making processes at local levels. For example, it is important to promote more actively the atmosphere of open competition and merit-based public service that would value the adoption of more innovative approaches and cost-effective solutions in e-government. The promotion of technology-driven public sector innovations and their procurement from non-governmental and private sectors could eventually contribute to the generation of better services in the area. In addition, in order to improve the quality of datasets that are generated at almost all institutional levels in public administration and ensure a systematic release of such information in machine-readable formats, e-government policymakers and practitioners may want to initiate a special public post of chief data officers (CDO) who would be politically responsible not only for the continuous flow of open data in government portals but also for the protection of personal data so that to minimize the chances for accidental publications of sensitive information. Every ministry and local municipality should have such CDOs. The same practice has been applied in government agencies in many US states since 2009 and recently become popular also in Europe, enriching the open data concept with new administrative mechanisms that could ensure better publication of government datasets. In this respect, the traditional FOIAs could not regulate all aspects of such work. Therefore, it is necessary to adopt more sophisticated regulatory mechanisms in the area, for example, by introducing new amendments to various legal acts and documents that regulate the protection of personal data, government and commercial secrets, use of electronic signatures and blockchain solutions in the area, etc. Moreover, it could also require new training courses for public servants who are directly working with various government datasets and documents, e.g., secretariats, registries, chancelleries, etc.

4.7.3 It Is Important to Promote the Grass-Root Participation in the Area

The key target audience of open data politics is citizenry since their active participation in the movement should be the first and foremost indicator of progress in the area. Citizens not only directly consume related digital services created by independent developers but also provide additional information and their own data to the platforms. Therefore, the political will and socioeconomic readiness of citizens to contribute is a crucial aspect of related public sector reforms. In this respect, it is necessary to note that the paradox in the development of open data and other related e-government concepts such as digital civic engagement, online crowd-sourcing, and e-participation is itself the traditional mind-set of both operators and citizenry in understanding how to realize and further the idea of open government data. For example, the ubiquitous "closed government culture" (Huijboom & Van den Broek, 2011) or no clear strategies on how to deal "with user input" (Janssen, Charalabidis, & Zuiderwijk, 2012) among government agents and lack of understanding on how to reuse the datasets among citizens, who usually play a role of passive consumers of various e-government services and products rather than as collaborators in their development, often impede the promotion of more independent mechanisms for open data-driven public sector reforms. In fact, the actual realization of any e-government ideas is usually very trivial and articulated in the straightforward executive directives (Linders & Wilson, 2011), i.e., administrative memorandums or mere declarations of intentions, when almost all projects are funded and implemented by the government itself or its subsidiary agencies, while the old top-down and one-way channel of implementation with practically no input from citizens is regarded as an accepted norm. As a result, paradoxically, the fundamentals of public administration remain the same; i.e., the old traditions of public service and public sector such as bureaucracy and red tape in its operation are the most challenging to reform due to the inertia in public mentality. In this regard, the obvious progress of the national e-government project and indirectly even of various related e-democracy platforms due to the further advance of the open data phenomena is more a by-product of a highly centralized and really relentless official e-government policy aimed at improving its innovative stance both domestically and, more importantly, globally rather than an ultimate political goal of the project itself. The implementation of the open data concept is regarded as one of the elements in building the e-government ecosystem, which itself, in turn, is part of a much-greater technological project such as informatization and industrial and infrastructural development of the country, where the overwhelming focus is paid to the socioeconomic aspects of promotion, including in raising publicity and public awareness in the area.

Policy recommendation

Nothing is impossible to a willing and open mind. Therefore, it is necessary for open data policymakers and practitioners in Kazakhstan to learn, network, and adopt the best practices in the area. In this respect, global cooperation and communication with counterparts from other countries as well as collaboration with the non-governmental sector could be extremely beneficial for all stakeholders of the open data movement. Such influential international intergovernmental and non-governmental organizations and consortiums as the United Nations Public Administration Network (UNPAN), the Open Government Partnership, the World Bank, and the Open Knowledge Foundation begin to play a very important role in globalizing the best e-government practices all over the world, especially in distributing universal standardized mechanisms on how to promote better open data-driven projects and start-ups. The indirect political demand of the international community to reform governance, at least digitally, all over the world makes the policymakers and entrepreneurs in many emerging nations, including Kazakhstan, to adopt the best implementation and operation models from the most developed countries and eventually promote the progressive ideas of transparency, collaboration, and participation. The e-government practitioners should realize that the open data concept is not only a tool to improve public administration and ensure greater transparency of government but also a promising socioeconomic platform that for its successful promotion requires today new ways of political communication and, more importantly, collaboration such as civic engagement and peer-to-peer digital participation. This could create new indirect incentives and opportunities to potentially democratize the fundamentals of the public domain through open data-driven projects and other e-government initiatives, regardless of economic and cultural contexts. Consequently, it is important to transform the traditional public mind-set in the area, especially among those who initiate and control open data reforms in public sector as well as those who are or should be regarded as target audiences, i.e., developers and citizens. Extensive public relations and public awareness campaigns in various mass media channels should become a number one source of outreaching in the area. After all, without concurrent changes in public mentality and understanding that open data is a modern way to promote civic engagement and participation, any related technology-driven public reforms could not be fully understood and successfully implemented. If the vast majority of decisions in public sector traditionally remain directive and top-down and any fulfillment of related strategic programs in the area in executive bodies are very formal and unquestioning, this could potentially lead to modest results or banal failures even despite the presence of the political will to succeed and strong economic capabilities of society to join and promote further open data politics at all institutional levels.

4.8 Summary: Understanding Key Findings of the Research

This chapter presents the review of open data policies and implementation strategies adopted by national authorities in Kazakhstan in the area. It also provides the close observation of political, economic, and social backgrounds that surround the open government movement in the context of this emerging economy that has recently adopted a special legislation on free access to information and is tentatively beginning to implement its own open data platforms in the area. The author presents his analysis as an empirical research, the results of which could be used by e-government scholars, practitioners, and policymakers in understanding the political and socioeconomic drivers and challenges of the open data movement in a typical transitional and post-totalitarian society, analyzing the interesting dynamics of professional networking activities that come into effect with the intensive advance of open data-driven projects throughout the country, and finally improving the operation of related e-government systems in many developing countries. Analyzing related regulatory acts, key political and socioeconomic incentives, main stakeholders and challenges in the diffusion of the open data phenomena, the author seeks to trace the emergence of participatory political culture that should accompany its development. In this regard, the key findings of the study suggests that open data provides new opportunities to promote civic engagement and e-participation but does not affect the fundamentals of political system nor advances traditional democratic institutions in a typical developing country, since the speed and ultimate goals of open data-driven transformations in political and socioeconomic domains do not necessarily correspond to each other. However, the recent adoption of the Kazakh FOIA and active implementation of various independent open data-driven projects, especially at the national level, which usually demand an increased participation from the members of civil society, sends a certain political signal to other stakeholders to join the movement, creating a promising platform for future progress in the area.

References

Ackerman, J. M., & Sandoval-Ballesteros, I. E. (2006). The global explosion of freedom of information laws. *Administrative Law Review*, 85–130.

AIITSH. (2018). *The Astana International IT and Startup Hub*. https://astanahub.com. Accessed on: September 27, 2018.

Åström, J., Karlsson, M., Linde, J., & Pirannejad, A. (2012). Understanding the rise of e-participation in non-democracies: Domestic and international factors. *Government Information Quarterly, 29*(2), 142–150.

Banisar, D. (2004). The Freedominfo. org Global Survey: Freedom of information and access to government record laws around the world.

BRC. (2017). *The business registration checker*. http://databay.kz/legal-entity. Accessed on: October 10, 2018.

Davies, T. G., & Bawa, Z. A. (2012). The promises and perils of open Government data (OGD). *The Journal of Community Informatics, 8*(2).
EDP. (2017). *The European Data Platform*. https://www.europeandataportal.eu. Accessed on: October 10, 2018.
Girish, J., Williams, C. B., & Yates, D. J. (2014). Predictors of on-line services and e-participation: A cross-national comparison. *Government Information Quarterly, 31*(4), 526–533.
Harrison, T. M., Pardo, T. A., & Cook, M. (2012). Creating open government ecosystems: A research and development agenda. *Future Internet, 4*(4), 900–928.
HCP. (2017). *The Healthcare open data-driven project*. https://itunes.apple.com/us/app/zdorov-e+-medicinskij-spravocnik/id1133507478?l=ru&ls=1&mt=8. Accessed on: October 10, 2018.
HDK. (2015). *The HackDay Kazakhstan Project*. http://hackday2015.kz. Accessed on: August 17, 2016.
Huijboom, N., & Van den Broek, T. (2011). Open data: An international comparison of strategies. *European journal of ePractice, 12*(1), 1–13.
ICT Fund. (2016). *The Infocommunication Development Fund of Kazakhstan*. www.ictfund.kz. Accessed on: May 4, 2017.
Information Kazakhstan—2020. (2013). *The Central Communications Service for the President of Kazakhstan*. http://ortcom.kz/en/program/program-infokaz/text/show. Accessed on: February 7, 2016.
Internet Live Stats. (2017b). *Kazakhstan Internet Users*. http://www.internetlivestats.com/internet-users/kazakhstan. Accessed on: May 18, 2018.
Janssen, M., Charalabidis, Y., & Zuiderwijk, A. (2012). Benefits, adoption barriers and myths of open data and open government. *Information systems management, 29*(4), 258–268.
Kassen, M. (2016). *E-government in Kazakhstan: A case study of multidimensional phenomena*. Routledge.
Kassen, M. (2018). Open data and its institutional ecosystems: A comparative cross-jurisdictional analysis of open data platforms. *Canadian Public Administration, 61*(1), 109–129.
Katz, J. M. (1969). Games bureaucrats play: Hide and seek under the freedom of information act. *Texas Law Review, 48*, 1261.
Kazakh, T. V. (2015). *Innovation week kicks off in Almaty*. http://kazakh-tv.kz/en/view/news_kazakhstan/page_132447_innovation-week-kicks-off-in-almaty. Accessed on: September 28, 2016.
Kazinform. (2015). *Week of innovations to be held in Kazakhstan Nov 9–13, 2015*. http://www.inform.kz/eng/article/2835333. Accessed on: August 5, 2016.
Law # 94-V. (2013). *The Kazakh law on personal data and their protection*. http://online.zakon.kz/Document/?doc_id=31396226#pos=1;-217. Accessed on: May 18, 2018.
Law # 401-V. (2015, November 2015). *The Kazakh law on access to information*. http://online.zakon.kz/Document/?doc_id=39415981. Accessed on: May 18, 2018.
Linders, D., & Wilson, S. C. (2011, June). What is open government? One year after the directive. In *Proceedings of the 12th Annual International Digital Government Research Conference: Digital Government Innovation in Challenging Times* (pp. 262–271). ACM.
LPRC. (2015). *The Legal Policy Research Centre*. http://lprc.kz/en/events/international_conference_access_to_information_and_public_participation_as_factor_of_ensuring_transparency_and_effectiveness_of_state_bodies-52.html. Accessed on: May 18, 2018.
Manley, L. (2015). Open Data for Business in Kazakhstan. *The World Bank*. http://blogs.worldbank.org/opendata/open-data-business-kazakhstan. Accessed on: September 28, 2016.
MID. (2016). *The Ministry of Investments and Development of Kazakhstan*. http://www.mid.gov.kz. Accessed on: August 31, 2018.
MOST. (2017). *The MOST business incubator*. http://most.com.kz/incubator. Accessed on: August 31, 2018.
NATD. (2016). *The National Agency for Technological Development*. http://natd.gov.kz. Accessed on: August 30, 2016.
NIT. (2016). *The National Information Technologies Agency*. www.nitec.kz. Accessed on: August 30, 2016.

Obi, T., & Iwasaki, N. (Eds.). (2015). *A decade of world E-Government rankings* (Vol. 7). IOS Press.

ODE. (2016). *The Open Data Europe Project*. https://open-data.europa.eu. Accessed on: September 5, 2016.

OECD. (2016). *OECD development pathways multi-dimensional review of Kazakhstan* (Vol. 1). Initial Assessment.

Orazgaliyeva, M. (2015, November 20). New law to give public greater access to government information. *The Astana Times*. http://astanatimes.com/2015/11/new-law-to-give-public-greater-access-to-government-information. Accessed on: September 28, 2016.

OSCE. (2015). *Opinion on the draft law on access to information of the republic of Kazakhstan and on related amendments to other legislative acts*. http://www.osce.org/odihr/164636?download=true. Accessed on: May 18, 2018.

PDP. (2017). *The public data project*. http://publicdata.eu. Accessed on: October 10, 2018.

SBP. (2016). *The startup battles projects*. http://techconnect.tech/startup-competition. Accessed on: May 15, 2017.

Stier, S. (2015). Political determinants of e-government performance revisited: Comparing democracies and autocracies. *Government Information Quarterly, 32*(3), 270–278.

TAP. (2017). *The TengeApp project*. https://itunes.apple.com/us/app/tengeapp-vidzety-s-aktual/id1107497979?l=ru&ls=1&mt=8. Accessed on: October 10, 2018.

TGP. (2016). *The Tech Garden Project* http://techgarden.kz. Accessed on: May 15, 2017.

The Constitution of Kazakhstan. (1998). http://www.parlam.kz/en/constitution. Accessed on: May 5, 2016.

The Electronic Government of Kazakhstan. (2015). *Open data round table*. http://egov.kz/wps/portal/Content?contentPath=/egovcontent/portalsnews/news/news_open_table&lang=en. Accessed on: September 5, 2016.

The Electronic Government of Kazakhstan. (2017). *Open Data Kazakhstan Hackathon*. http://egov.kz/cms/en/news/Hakaton-Open-Data-Kazakhstan. Accessed on: September 27, 2018.

The Open Data 500 Global Network. (2015). http://www.opendata500.com/. Accessed on: September 5, 2016.

The Open Data Project of Kazakhstan. (2017). http://data.egov.kz/. Accessed on: March 14, 2018.

The Strategy 2050. (2015). https://strategy2050.kz/en/news/28501/. Accessed on: May 18, 2018.

The Techconnect Project. (2015). http://techconnect.tech/blog/astex-2015-at-techconnect-astana. Accessed on: September 5, 2016.

The Tedxastana Project. (2015). http://tedxastana.com Accessed on: August 17, 2016.

Trading Economics. (2017). *The trading economics platform*. http://www.tradingeconomics.com/kazakhstan/indicators. Accessed on: March 14, 2018.

UNESCO. (2017). *Country Profile: Kazakhstan*. http://www.unesco.org/uil/litbase/?menu=15&programme=118. Accessed on: March 14, 2018.

UNPAN. (2003). *The global E-government survey*. United Nations Public Administration Network. http://unpan3.un.org/egovkb/en-us/Reports/UN-E-Government-Survey-2003. Accessed on: March 25, 2018.

UNPAN. (2004). *The global E-government readiness report. Towards access for opportunity*. http://unpan1.un.org/intradoc/groups/public/documents/un/unpan019207.pdf. Accessed on: April 19, 2018.

UNPAN. (2005). *The global E-government readiness report. From e-Government to e-Inclusion*. http://unpan1.un.org/intradoc/groups/public/documents/un/unpan021888.pdf. Accessed on: April 19, 2018.

UNPAN. (2008). *The global E-government survey. From E-government to connected governance*. http://unpan1.un.org/intradoc/groups/public/documents/un/unpan028607.pdf. Accessed on: April 19, 2018.

UNPAN. (2010). *The global E-government survey. Leveraging E-government at a time of financial and economic crisis*. http://www2.unpan.org/egovkb/global_reports/10report.htm. Accessed on: April 19, 2018.

UNPAN. (2012). *The global E-government survey. E-government for the people*. http://unpan3.un.org/egovkb/Portals/egovkb/Documents/un/2012-Survey/unpan048065.pdf. Accessed on: April 19, 2018.

UNPAN. (2014). *The global E-government survey. E-government for the future we want*. http://unpan3.un.org/egovkb/Reports/UN-E-Government-Survey-2014. Accessed on: April 19, 2018.

UNPAN. (2016). *The global E-government survey. E-government in support of sustainable development*. https://publicadministration.un.org/egovkb/en-us/reports/un-e-government-survey-2016. Accessed on: April 19, 2018.

UNPAN. (2018). The global E-government survey: gearing E-government to support transformation towards sustainable and resilient societies https://publicadministration.un.org/egovkb/en-us/Reports/UN-E-Government-Survey-2018. Accessed on: November 17, 2018.

Wald, P. M. (1984). Freedom of information act: A short case study in the perils and paybacks of legislating democratic values. *The Emory Lj, 33,* 649.

WJP. (2017). *The world justice project*. http://data.worldjusticeproject.org. Accessed on: March 14, 2018.

World Bank. (2017). *Country Profile: Kazakhstan*. http://data.worldbank.org/country/kazakhstan. Accessed on: March 14, 2018.

Yvision. (2011). *The Yvision project*. http://samsungkz.yvision.kz/post/196360. Accessed on: September 5, 2016.

Zerde. (2015). *The Kazakh National Infocommunication holding*. www.zerde.gov.kz/en/kholding.html.

Chapter 5
Political and Socioeconomic Implications of Open Data Politics

5.1 The Promotion of Open Data Politics Changes Traditional E-Government Philosophy

The key finding of the case study research suggests that the concept of open data, provided that it is fulfilled in an intrinsically collaborative manner, could potentially change the course of technology-driven public sector reforms. Furthermore, it could also transform traditional dynamics of related networking activities among its key stakeholders both public and private, which until recently have usually been reflected in a top-down endorsement of e-governance by the public sector as the most effective instrument of implementation. In this respect, the further development of open data politics could over time become a synonym of such e-government reforms since citizens themselves could play a more important role in the processes. The participation of the public sector could eventually be diminished only to a mere administrative role of datasets provider. Civic engagement and indirect participation of private and non-governmental sectors are a true political and socioeconomic driver of the movement. For example, if the main products and services of e-government reforms today are traditionally provided by only public sector itself in a strictly directive manner even in the most democratic political contexts and paradoxically with almost zero participation of private and non-governmental sectors, then the full realization of the open data concept by local civic communities and promotion of related public sector reforms by government will be much more collaborative, transparent, and, probably, cost-effective enterprise, since all stakeholders could now participate in the development of open data-driven projects and create new services independently.

The public value of open data philosophy is the fact not only that it demands the presence of developed democratic institutions and individual freedoms as a political prerequisite to support various civic start-ups and initiatives in the area but also that it promises to increase significantly networking and participation of citizens in related decision-making processes, providing a really effective ideological platform

M. Kassen, *Open Data Politics*, SpringerBriefs in Political Science,
https://doi.org/10.1007/978-3-030-11410-7_5

to boost egalitarianism in its most direct form. The promotion of e-government systems is traditionally associated with the advance of digital democracy, even despite the fact that often public sector itself initiates, develops, and operates such digital systems and the situation with the intrinsically crucial role of central government in the processes is regarded as an accepted norm. After all, it is a usual implementation mechanism in all other technology-driven public sector reforms in a representative democracy such as e-voting, e-procurement, e-taxing, and e-legislation. Even the promotion of e-participation practices, arguably the most democratic method to advance digital government in any administrative contexts, implies again the use of electronic systems developed by public sector itself. In this regard, the idea of open data could dramatically transform the established traditions of e-government building philosophy, turning it into a truly collaborative phenomenon with an extremely wide range of networking trends and dynamically changing roles among its stakeholders. Indeed, as the close analysis of open data politics in both Estonia and Kazakhstan demonstrates, the effective results in the area could be achieved only if e-government policymakers and independent developers begin to cooperate and collaborate actively in promoting the concept. Furthermore, the full realization of the open data concept is not possible without the direct participation of citizens in providing additional information and, more importantly, priceless feedback through such collaborative projects.

5.2 Open Data as a Context Dependable Phenomenon

The case study research in each of the two observed nations has also illustrated that the development of open government data is a really complex and manifold phenomenon in which advancement as a sustainable concept of public sector reforms becomes possible only if there is a right combination of political and socioeconomic conditions for the successful promotion of its main public values among all stakeholders, i.e., transparency, participation, and collaboration. In this respect, the political readiness of national authorities to promote the open government agenda at different institutional levels on the one hand and socioeconomic capability of civil society to hear the political signals, which are calling to adopt and advance further the concept, is what made the practical implementation of open data politics, regardless of their different contexts, possible in these cases. However, the degree of civic reaction to these signals and scale of participation in the movement may vary, perhaps, reflecting different political, historical, and more importantly, socioeconomic preconditions in adopting open data philosophy among, first, those who are at the forefront of the movement, that is, developers and technically savvy citizens. Independent developers, whose participation in the processes is usually obscured and invisible to onlookers, are a crucial component of an open data movement, and the more socioeconomically they are interested to join it and, more importantly, ready to develop such projects, the more advanced the society is on its road to build an open data-driven economy and government.

In general, the promotion of open government philosophy, which ideally should be reflected in an explosive growth of open data-driven start-ups in a wide range of areas, becomes more successful when all favorable preconditions and drivers are readily available to support open data agenda in all its contexts, i.e., *political* (e.g., the strong traditions of freedom of information legislation, popularity of e-government agendas at all institutional levels both national and local, active promotion of public awareness policies in the area, etc.), *economic* (e.g., the presence of developed local economy, infrastructural readiness, high level of Internet penetration and low level of digital divide, promotion of ICT and other technical majors in institutions of tertiary education, etc.), and *social contexts* (e.g., the socially active neighborhoods, traditions of civic engagement, popularity of voluntarism and sense of keenness among key stakeholders, first of all, developers and e-government enthusiasts to support their local communities with the help of new open data-driven services, etc.). In this regard, the political and economic

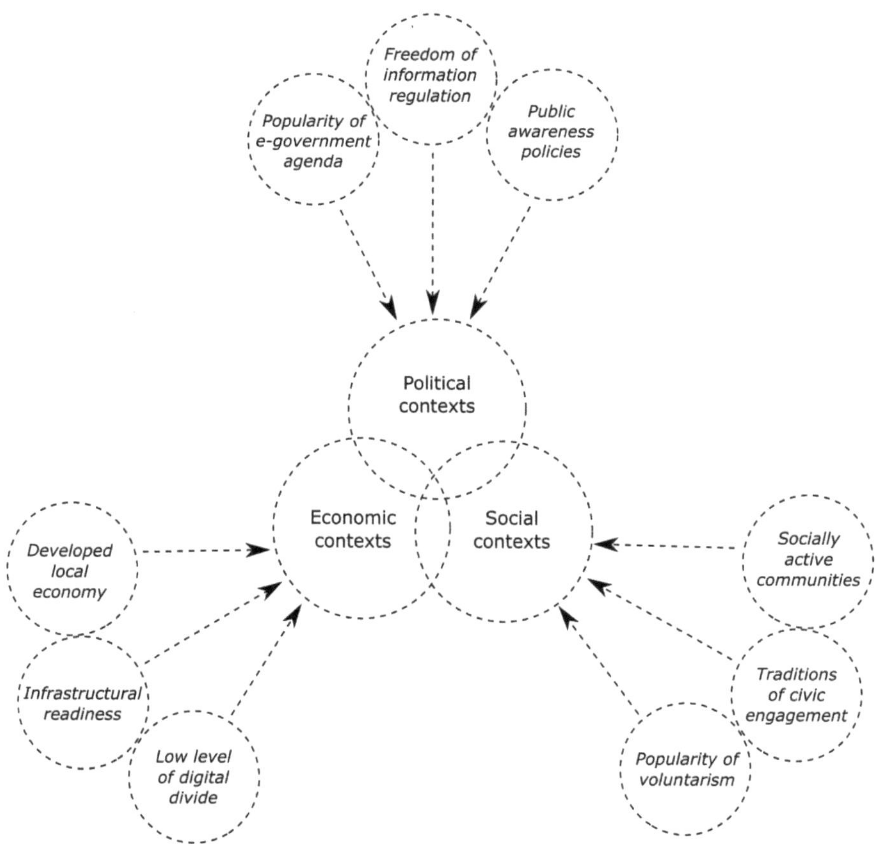

Fig. 5.1 The key political and socioeconomic drivers of the open data movement. *Source* Own illustration

capability of civil society to join the movement and philanthropic feelings of its individual members play a crucial role in the processes (see Fig. 5.1).

For example, in case of Estonia, the presence of developed social welfare economy as a result of adherence to social democracy has played an important role in providing favorable political and, more importantly, socioeconomic environment for the emergence of an extremely wide range of open data-driven projects and peer-to-peer start-ups, in which development and promotion is *systematically supported by individual members of civil society.* The fundamental pillars of open society such as established traditions of civic engagement, public–private partnerships and participation as well as strong traditions of social democracy, which truly values the ideas of social justice and decidedly curbs the most controversial and inhumane aspects of capitalism, helped this Baltic nation to succeed tremendously in this direction. Moreover, in both Estonia and Kazakhstan, the overall popularity of e-government agendas in local politics and the presence of an extremely interconnected community of independent developers such as designers, coders, software testers, and other specialists in computer industries provided favorable political and socioeconomic conditions to advance the open data movement in these transitional societies, even in a less developed economic context. Often driven by professional curiosity and patriotic feelings, independent developers are ready to help their neighborhoods to thrive and prosper with various digital solutions often on a philanthropic basis.

In general, it is interesting to note that the promotion of open data agendas in politics allowed to create a really conducive soil to advance the concept of open government among most economically independent and socially active individuals. These technologically savvy people who often call themselves open data enthusiasts represent an army of specialists from various professions and backgrounds (software developers, computer gurus, system administrators, startup entrepreneurs, data journalists, public activists, lobbying groups, students of polytechnic universities, etc.). It is this sense of social progressivism and active civic stance that is intrinsically embedded in the collective mind-set of local communities that helps to create strong open data-driven societies, which allows to closely monitor government activity in various areas through open data-driven civic start-ups and, more importantly, indirectly sending back to public sector the political signals in what kind of social issues they are mostly concerned, whether it is observing electronically the nuances of local budget planning, public spending, crime rate mapping, solving challenges of transportation or regional economic development, etc. In this connection, actively promoting various independent collaborative and communicational platforms in the area, these two nations quickly realized the political and economic promise of open government politics, which was offered conceptually by the Obama administration in early 2009, especially in furthering one of its most crucial elements—open data philosophy. In this regard, individual members of civil society, technically savvy citizens, independent developers and e-government experts as well as freelance journalists and representatives of non-governmental organizations are the true heroes of the open data movement. They are ready to contribute and create an extremely wide range of civic open data-driven projects and initiatives aimed at advancing socioeconomic development of their local communities.

5.3 Open Data—It Is All About Collaboration and Networking Among Stakeholders

As the case studies of actual independent open data projects in both Estonia and Kazakhstan have demonstrated, their technological implementation has always been organizationally accompanied by the birth of new networking and collaborative connections between various stakeholders. Indeed, in order to successfully launch and operate such projects, it is necessary, first of all, to ensure a close, mutually beneficial and systematic cooperation among those who promote the publication and reuse of government datasets, i.e., policymakers, practitioners, and developers, and their main target audiences, i.e., citizens and businesses who, as a result, could begin to receive new digital services and information from such collaborative start-ups. In this regard, developers apparently play a crucial role of a certain technological bridge between all stakeholders of the open data movement, working mainly on its own initiative and often driven by pure enthusiasm and professional curiosity and only occasionally receiving some support from local non-governmental and business sectors. For the business sector, the concept offers a great opportunity to boost the public–private partnership with local governments in advancing together joint e-commerce projects and maintaining related corporate platforms. For the non-governmental sector and media communities, the participation in advancing open data-driven projects could provide, respectively, a new ideological platform to promote transparent and collaborative government and an additional opportunity to build new channels of public relations in the area with both government agencies and citizens. Such collaboration also promises some practical dividends for local journalists, especially in using various government datasets for their analytical reports, investigations, and surveys. Therefore, the development of open data-driven projects itself could be regarded as quite an effective social instrument to boost networking between representatives of both the public and private sectors of the local economy.

Another finding suggests that open government from the perspective of peers might be regarded not necessarily as a platform for government-related transactions but as a source of information or even raw material for other digital products, for example, in case of open data, for various third-party e-government projects and initiatives. Therefore, the active implementation and further promotion of these intrinsically independent open data-driven systems and related interactive platforms could conceptually undermine the traditional monopoly of the public sector. In developing such digital platforms, e-government policymakers break the established black box mentality, especially in regard to the widely accepted understanding of e-government philosophy as an official-only enterprise. This potentially could transform the whole concept with new participatory and civic engagement dimensions to further the very political agenda of digital government in a much more transparent and collaborative manner. Thus, for the first time in the history of e-government philosophy, related public sector services could now be created and promoted outside of its traditional implementation realm due to public–private partnerships in the area, eventually helping to develop a sustainable universal paradigm of the concept promotion in the future. In this regard, it is necessary to note that as it was observed in all cases, open data philosophy always demands cooperation and collaboration among practitioners in the public sector on the one hand and stakeholders from the private sector on the other. Thus, the open data movement has more chances to be successful only if the former are ready to network and participate.

5.4 Open Data Transforms Freedom of Information Regulation Traditions

The analysis of regulation policies adopted in these two nations shows that the freedom of information act (FOIA) is the most important document that regulates almost all aspects of public access to government files and other related public release of official information in all sectors of economy. It is also often applied in a legal sense to the publication of various machine-readable datasets, i.e., in the area of government activity that eventually results in a systematic publication of updateable open data in special public depositories and portals. In this respect, in all observed cases, such national documents with all necessary amendments associated with the promotion of open data practices in an interactive digital manner have played a crucial role in regulating legally the open data movement as, first of all, collaborative phenomena. All related texts unambiguously indicate to certain promising political, economic, and social values of reusing the datasets in private and non-governmental sectors of national economy, highlighting new opportunities for various third-party initiatives and start-ups in the area.

The paradox of the open data regulation is that it provides a new conceptual ground to revise itself a traditional understanding of FOIA as a *reactive* legal phenomenon. The public release of government datasets is not a bureaucratic procedure anymore, which usually provides private access to such documents in an on-demand basis. It is a new administrative practice that requires almost all government agencies to publish such information in the most transparent and, more importantly, *proactive* manner. Also, in addition to traditional laws in the area that directly institutionalized the public release of government information, each observed nation has also adopted special legal acts that proclaimed a universal right of citizens to access various public documents and records in machine-readable forms.

5.5 The Reuse of Open Data Demands More Sustainable Mechanism of Promotion

As it was observed in each of the individual national cases, the development of various open data-driven projects and related civic initiatives also offers a really cost-effective platform to boost public sector innovations and new business models in networking e-government practitioners, entrepreneurs, and developers, turning the concept of open government from mainly enthusiastic and civic-driven movement into a profitable commercial mechanism that could generate new business products and services in the private sector, too. Both government and corporate sectors in each country pay special attention to the promotion of commercial start-ups that could help to develop sustainable business models in the area. These stakeholders clearly understand that the concept could not be advanced only on the promise of civic engagement, philanthropic feelings, and professional curiosity of independent developers or voluntarism of non-governmental players. These drivers of open data movement are important for the promotion of the concept in civil society, but it is necessary to understand that it is not a sustainable way to further the philosophy of open government.

The long-term technological support of open data-driven projects is a time- and money-consuming undertaking. Therefore, the development of systematic and cost-effective approaches should be viewed as much needed in the area. The open data concept is coming of age, and it could potentially offer great opportunities to boost national economies thanks to an increasingly higher level of transparency and provision of better communication channels with the government sector. Furthermore, as a mechanism of public sector innovations, it could help to propagate data-driven economy, where the successful development of independent projects in the area is guaranteed only if there is a strong will of all stakeholders to cooperate and collaborate. In this respect, new business models to promote the creation of a chain of semi-products for developers and non-governmental players could provide an additional motivation to boost the open data movement in a more sustainable and systematic manner.

5.6 Centralization Trends in Generating Open Data Depositories

The regional institutional perspective in organizing government open data portals is as a relatively new dimension of open data-driven communication due to the fact that there are not so many really successful examples of political integration between countries that results in the development of single centralized open government strategies or, at least, universal implementation instruments and single laws in the area. The ideal example of this type of transactions might be open government networks that exist today in the European Union, which are promoted especially between such actors as, for example, regional open government platforms on the one hand and national and even local players on the other (e.g., in indicating transactions between the open data portals situated in Brussels, i.e., in the administrative capital of the union and residents or business entities who live at local levels, e.g., somewhere in remote areas of Saaremaa in Estonia). This phenomenon could be tentatively called as electronic confederalism or *e-confederalism* in contrast to *e-federalism* and *e-centralism* that conceptually exist today, respectively, in federal and unitary states. Even though this type of open government transactions is not so popular in the world, taking into account that the EU is, probably, the only successful example of such close regional political and economic integration, the increasing popularity of the idea to integrate national open government projects and databases into single supra-government open data platforms in some parts of the world, hypothetically, in North America (e.g., at the regional cross-border levels between the USA, Canada, and Mexico), Latin America, the Arab World, Eurasian Union, and other parts of the world could create a new institutional dimension to promote regional open government networks on the model of the European supranational public institutions that already exist and are actively propagated, transforming the concept into geographically multidimensional phenomena.

For example, the implementation of such open data platforms in the USA as data.gov in national government, data.illinois.gov in the State of Illinois, data.-cookcounty.gov in the Cook County, Illinois and data.cityofchicago.org in the City of Chicago, which are realized, respectively, *at federal, state, provincial,* and *local levels* shapes a truly multi-institutional realm of the open government movement in this federal nation, which results in the promotion of a really diverse array of implementation strategies and tactics in the area. In this regard, the development of the open data movement in these two unitary states could be characterized as one-dimensional. It is based on the implementation of the single open government platform, using centralized government databases. This trend is reflected in the emergence of such quite a rare e-government phenomenon as digital centralism or e-centralism. For example, citizens, who live in such local towns as Karkaraly in Karaganda province or Zaisan in East Kazakhstan region and in the capital city of Astana, have single access to a highly centralized system of digital government such as egov.kz, which also hosts a single open data depositary—data.egov.kz (see Fig. 5.2). In this respect, the promotion of open data platforms could be extremely cost-effective even in a less favorable political and socioeconomic context of a transitional society if the principle of centralization is used in a systematic manner in generating single inter-institutional datasets.

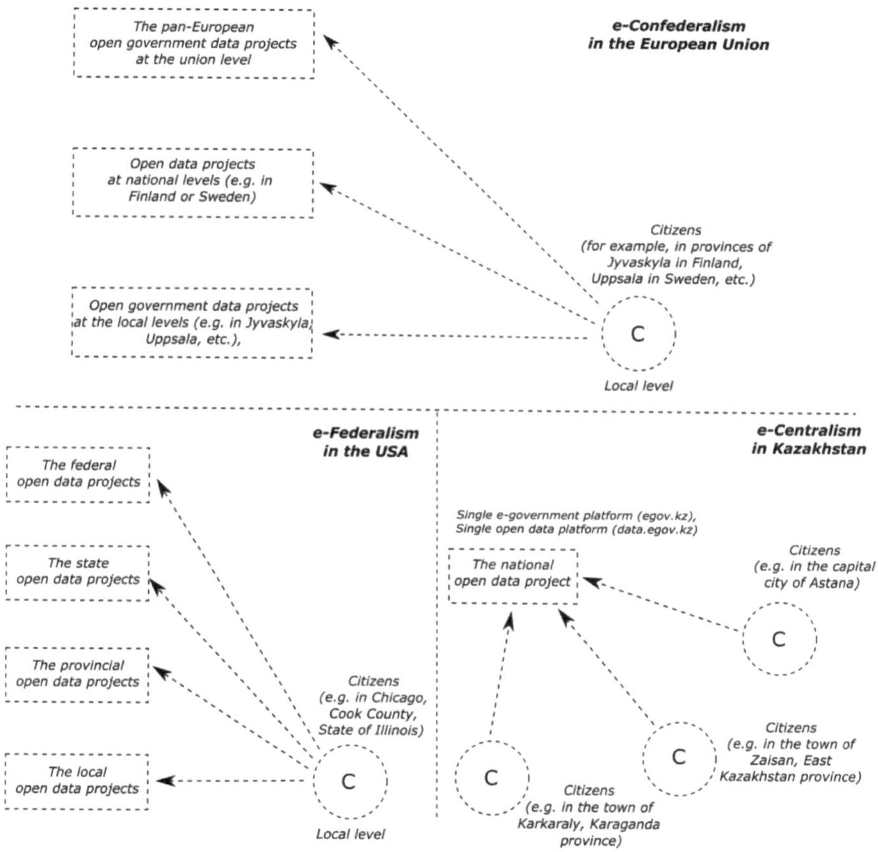

Fig. 5.2 Understanding key institutional trends in advancing open data platforms. *Source* Own illustration

5.7 Public Relations Campaigns Is Instrumental in Promoting Open Data Philosophy Among Potential Stakeholders

As it was observed in all cases, the advocacy of open data politics is often accompanied with extensive media campaigns and public relations events in popular social networks that not only help to raise public awareness about the phenomena, potentially increasing the number of ultimate clients for various collaborative, citizen-sourcing projects and related independent open data-driven initiatives, but also draw a professional and commercial interest from an army of independent developers and entrepreneurs. These specialists and business people themselves are beginning to cooperate with both government agencies and, more importantly, each other, developing a wide community of open data projects.

These independent journalistic and expert communities often convene and communicate on a regular basis through various professional meetings and hackathons in order to contest, learn, share, and show off their best solutions in the area and sometimes even to find additional funding or assistance (consultative, technical, or media) to their prospective open data-driven projects and related crowdsourcing platforms. This eventually creates new niches for economic and fundraising activities. Again and again, all stakeholders should remember that *open data politics is all about transparency, participation, and collaboration*, the slogan that truly drives almost all related networking activities in the area. In this regard, the organization of such media campaigns is also often a popular venue for various think tanks, activist movements, academic institutions and, more importantly, non-governmental organizations and philanthropic groups to network with various stakeholders and support promising business ideas or existing start-ups.

Conclusion

The main practical contribution of the book is that it provides a detailed review of open data politics in two transitional countries such as Estonia and Kazakhstan, which could be especially helpful for policymakers in evaluating and improving the work of various open data-driven public sector projects. One more practical contribution of the research is a number of policy recommendations that the author presents in his work for e-government practitioners and project managers in solving various challenges in a wide range of open data platforms and related digital initiatives. In this regard, the chapters number three and four provide a concrete set of advices on how to improve administratively, economically and politically the operation of various open data and, more importantly, open data-driven civic initiatives. The author also elaborates on the potential emergence of new road-blocks that may impede the development of the concept in transitional countries such, for example, as the paradoxical competition between e-government and open data ecosystems, the lack of open data-driven projects in advancing the concept in its political dimension, no collaboration with business sector in promoting such projects and finally, the apathy of traditional public mentality and indifference of bureaucratic machine on how to deal with civic input and various organizational and technological barriers in the area.

In general, the results of the research could be used by e-government policymakers and practitioners in evaluating and improving the operation of various open data-driven platforms all over the world, providing a multidimensional perspective on the development of this phenomenon, especially taking into account that it is analyzed in the context of two transitional economies and, institutionally, at different levels of government. The book is presented as a policy review research, which could be interesting for a global community of open data experts, e-government specialists, political scientists, journalists, lawyers, computer developers, business persons and all those who are interested in studying this political and socioeconomic phenomenon. Open data politics is a new phenomenon, which could affect many aspects of human activity and change the traditional understanding of technology-driven public sector reforms. In this regard, the book is also

M. Kassen, *Open Data Politics*, SpringerBriefs in Political Science,
https://doi.org/10.1007/978-3-030-11410-7

intended as an introduction to this emerging concept from empirical perspectives and will be ideal for various practical trainings in business environment and government agencies as well as academic courses as a material for collateral reading in public policy and public administration studies.

Bibliography

Akyürek, H., Scholl, C., Stodden, R., Siebenlist, T., & Mainka, A. (2018). Maturity and usability of open data in North Rhine-Westphalia. In *Proceedings of the 19th Annual International Conference on Digital Government Research: Governance in the Data Age* (p. 18). ACM.

Esteve Casellas Serra, L. (2014). The mapping, selecting and opening of data: The records management contribution to the Open Data project in Girona City Council. *Records Management Journal, 24*(2), 87–98.

Janssen, K. (2012). Open government data and the right to information: Opportunities and obstacles. *The Journal of Community Informatics, 8*(2).

Khan, G. F. (2015). The Government 2.0 utilization model and implementation scenarios. *Information Development, 31*(2), 135–149.

MEAC. (2018). *The Ministry of Economic Affairs and Communications*. https://www.mkm.ee/en. Accessed on: November 24, 2018.

OECD. (2015). *OECD public governance reviews: Estonia and Finland: Fostering strategic capacity across government and digital services across borders*. OECD Publishing Paris.

Praxis. (2018). *The Praxis Think Tank.* http://www.praxis.ee/en. Accessed on: November 24, 2018.

M. Kassen, *Open Data Politics*, SpringerBriefs in Political Science,
https://doi.org/10.1007/978-3-030-11410-7

MIX
Papier aus verantwortungsvollen Quellen
Paper from responsible sources
FSC® C105338

If you have any concerns about our products,
you can contact us on
ProductSafety@springernature.com

In case Publisher is established outside the EU,
the EU authorized representative is:
Springer Nature Customer Service Center GmbH
Europaplatz 3, 69115 Heidelberg, Germany

Printed by Libri Plureos GmbH
in Hamburg, Germany